Time Is a Plant

Critical Plant Studies

PHILOSOPHY, LITERATURE, CULTURE

Series Editor

Michael Marder
(*IKERBASQUE/The University of the Basque Country, Vitoria*)

VOLUME 7

Time Is a Plant

By

Michael Marder

BRILL

LEIDEN | BOSTON

Cover image: Evgenia Emets, "Peregrination / Peregrinação," *Coffea arabica*, from the *Forest Time / Religar* series, watercolor on paper, 2023.

This book has been financially supported by GAIT, the Basque Government research group on "Social change, emerging forms of subjectivity and identity in contemporary societies" (IT1469-22).]

GAIT·CEIC

Library of Congress Cataloging-in-Publication Data

Names: Marder, Michael, 1980- author.
Title: Time is a plant / by Michael Marder.
Description: Boston, Massachusetts : Brill, [2023] | Series: Critical plant studies, 2213-0659 ; vol 7 | Includes bibliographical references and index.
Identifiers: LCCN 2023032679 (print) | LCCN 2023032680 (ebook) | ISBN 9789004679887 (paperback) | ISBN 9789004679894 (ebook)
Subjects: LCSH: Plants (Philosophy) | Time–Philosophy | Philosophy of nature.
Classification: LCC B105.P535 M38 2023 (print) | LCC B105.P535 (ebook) | DDC 113–dc23/eng/20230905
LC record available at https://lccn.loc.gov/2023032679
LC ebook record available at https://lccn.loc.gov/2023032680

Typeface for the Latin, Greek, and Cyrillic scripts: "Brill". See and download: brill.com/brill-typeface.

ISSN 2213-0659
ISBN 978-90-04-67988-7 (paperback)
ISBN 978-90-04-67989-4 (e-book)

For Eli, my fabulous φυτόν

∵

If you can look into the seeds of time
And say which grain will grow and which will not,
Speak, then, to me, who neither beg nor fear
Your favors nor your hate.

WILLIAM SHAKESPEARE, *Macbeth*, Act I, Scene 3.

∵

Contents

Acknowledgements

An early, short version of the text at the core of chapter 2 was published as "The Weirdness of Being in Time: Aristotle, Hegel, and Plants" in *Philosophy and Rhetoric*, 54(4), 2021, pp. 333–347. Chapter 3, "Cosmic [Tree] Time," appeared as a contribution to the book, *Notes on Ex-Futures*, edited by Johanna Gustafsson Fürst and Asier Mendizabal (Stockholm: Praun & Guermouche, 2023). This book has been financially supported by GAIT, the Basque Government research group on "Social change, emerging forms of subjectivity, and identity in contemporary societies" (IT1469-22) to which I belong. I thank Erika Mandarino and Helena Schöb of Brill for their unwaivering support for this project and the book series as a whole. With this, I hand *Time Is a Plant* back to time and to plants, by publishing the work, by making it publically visible—a visibility that nevertheless remains ensconced in the obscurity of everything that made it possible.

GAIT·CEIC

Incipit: Adventures in the Vegetality of Time

We are used to picturing time as a succession of instants. Debates may rage as to whether this succession is arranged in an arrow, in a circle, or in a jagged line more uneven than either of these representations. If time is an arrow, then its trajectory, rushing from the past toward the future, will tend upward (spelling out progress), downward (indicating decline), or horizontally (as an indifferent continuum signaling homeostasis). If it completes a circle, then time is cyclical or spiraling, with various events, phases, ascents and descents repeated at more or less regular intervals.

Whether an arrow, a circle, or a squiggle, the view of time in historical imagination and in everyday life relies on lines and figures, the elements of geometry that are, properly speaking, spatial. From some philosophical quarters, criticism has been leveled against the "impure" or "inauthentic" schematization of time that spuriously resorts to geometrical and, hence, non-temporal categories. Even so, this way of imagining does not go beyond the limits of abstract patterns, drawn from a series of events, rarefied and disembodied. Immanuel Kant was more radical than that. Although he took it for granted that time necessarily involved a succession, rather than simultaneity, Kant argued that it was "not an empirical concept that is somehow drawn from experience [*kein empirischer Begriff, der irgend von einer Erfahrung abgezogen worden*]" (*CPR* B46) and that it is "given *a priori*. In it alone is all actuality of appearances possible. The latter could all disappear, but time itself (as the universal condition of their possibility) cannot be removed" (*CPR* A31).[1]

As a universal condition of the possibility of all appearances, time itself cannot be an appearance, not even one as bare-boned as a geometrical figure or a line. Everything that appears in time then disappears (and may eventually disappear as a whole, bowing to the power and primacy of the atemporal, the eternal: philosophers had been fond of imagining total devastation, which is the truiumph of eternal being or non-being, still before the technical means to accomplish this feat were developed), but time itself is both inapparent and indestructible. In his philosophical system, Kant elaborates Isaac Newton's conception of time, notably of absolute time, complementary to absolute space: mathematically expressible, uniform, abstract, unaffected by

---

1 References to Kant's *Critique of Pure Reason* appear in brackets, containing the pagination of the first (A) or second (B) editions. The English translation used is Immanuel Kant, *Critique of Pure Reason (The Cambridge Edition of the Works of Immanuel Kant)*, edited and translated by Paul Guyer and Allen W. Wood (Cambridge: Cambridge University Press, 1999).

any external objects that are *in* time or *in* space. Which means that the under-cutting of Newtonian physics would also invalidate the philosophical notion of time that proceeds from the same scientific paradigm.

With Albert Einstein's theory of relativity, time (or, more precisely, space-time) is no longer an absolute, transcendental, *a priori* given. Time measure-ments *Y* are dependent on the "inertial system *K*" in the vicinity of which they are conducted: "With clocks so adjusted, we can assign the time to events which take place near any one of them. It is essential to note that this defi-nition of time relates only to the intertial system *K*, since we have used a sys-tem of clocks at rest relatively to *K*. The assumption which was made in the pre-relativity physics of the absolute character of time (i.e. the independence of time of the choice of the inertial system) does not follow at all from this definition."[2] More importantly, time is not empty; as I put it in *Energy Dreams* apropos of relativity theory, "energy and mass, the two modes of appearing belonging to the same reality, do not occur in preexistent space and time but, depending on their densities, alignments, and distributions, modify the expe-rience of spacetime."[3] There is nothing wrong with space-based articulations of time; actually, conventional circles and lines, in which time sequences are arranged, are half-measures, rendering uniform and idealizing the uneven, multifarious, dispersed distributions of energy. We should go further than that with the spatialization of time, experimenting with its diverse configurations.

Time becomes much more concrete right before our eyes; it is, Einstein avers, of "a physically real, and not a mere[ly] fictitious, significance."[4] (Note that *concrete*, despite its apparent hardness, already leads us to the vegetal world of growing-with, *com-crescere*).[5] A sequence relies on the experience of sequen-tially given things. Time is not only imaginable as, but it also really exists in shapes, figures, figurations, or configurations that are irreducible to figurative notions, holding what Einstein calls a "merely fictitious significance." A com-ing to visibility and a drifting out of visibility, it is of a piece with the kind of world that unfolds in time and that, if we are to be consistent with the critique of Newtonian-Kantian philosophy launched by the theory of relativity, is tied to the fate of that world.

2   Albert Einstein, *The Meaning of Relativity* (London & New York: Routledge, 2003), p. 28.
3   Michael Marder, *Energy Dreams: Of Actuality* (New York: Columbia University Press, 2017),
     p. 155. Einstein directs an implicit rebuke to Kant when he writes: "I am convinced that the
     philosophers have had a harmful effect upon the progress of scientific thinking in removing
     certain fundamental concepts from the domain of empiricism, where they are under our
     control, to the intangible heights of the *a priori*" (*The Meaning of Relativity*, p. 2).
4   Einstein, *The Meaning of Relativity*, p. 29.
5   I thank Marcia Sá Cavalcante Schuback for this insight.

"Our" world, in turn, is without fail vegetal. None of it would have been in existence were it not for the life activity of plants. Time, discernible in the rhythms, intervals, logics, articulations and disarticulations of the world, is the time of plants. Where these diverge from vegetal processes, we *either* face the possibility of world-collapse, a certain un-worlding and un-timing of the world announced in the current climate breakdown, *or* affirm and maintain alternative temporalities in tacit opposition to plants, though such an opposition may, at a deeper level, reveal itself as a mutation within vegetal time and its processes of growth, decay, and metamorphosis. That is to say—in case we are still willing to preserve something of the Kantian philosophical heritage—contemplating time and space, as the conditions of possibility for experience grouped in "The Transcendental Aesthetic" section of Kant's *First Critique*, we come face-to-face (or, better yet, face-to-surface, or surface-to-surface) with **the vegetal** *a priori*.

In *Plant-Thinking*, I outlined different senses of the time of plants, ranging from vegetal hetero-temporalities to the "bad infinity" of growth and the iterability of expression.[6] What is at stake now is the vegetality of time as such, or, more colloquially, the assertion made in the very title of the present study that time is a plant and the thesis that the time of plants is the temporality of time. With the issue of time's figuration already addressed, if not resolved, an immediate rejoinder to this thesis is that, although the livable world on this planet is shaped by plants, this does not hold for the rest of the cosmos. Until scientific proofs to the contrary emerge, it is incontrovertible that plants are a terrestrial lifeform and, therefore, do not rise to the universality that "as such" presupposes. How, then, is it possible to sustain the argument about the vegetality of time?

The hetero-temporality of plants I discussed in *Plant-Thinking* is galvanized by the time of the other—the inorganic, animal, fungal, bacterial, elemental, stellar, or solar other of plants. In other words, the time of plants is indissociable from the temporality of non-vegetal entities and processes. Adjusting our theoretical vision to the cosmic level, we cannot help but notice that, across cultures, the universe beyond our planet is contemplated as a cosmic tree, its time acquiring the same vegetal feel as its shape. I venture into this topic in chapter 3 of the book. Mircea Eliade comments on the cosmic tree in his *Patterns of Comparative Religion*: "By simply being there ('power') and by its natural laws of development ('regeneration'), the tree re-enacts what, to the primitive understanding, *is* the whole cosmos. The tree can, of course, become

---

6   Michael Marder, *Plant-Thinking: A Philosophy of Vegetal Life* (New York: Columbia University Press, 2013), pp. 93–117.

a *symbol* of the universe, and in that form we find it in more developed civilizations; but to a primitive religious mind, the tree *is* the universe, and it *is* so because it reproduces it and as it were sums it up as well as 'symbolizing' it."[7] My suggestion, nonetheless, is to return to what Eliade all too brusquely rejects as "primitive understanding" and to allow that the tree *is* the universe, rather than its symbol. Then, not only the shape but also the time of the universe would be tree-time.

It is not by chance that "Cosmic [Tree] Time" is a pivotal chapter, the exact middle around which the rest of the book you are now reading revolves, just as the cosmic tree, a pivot in its own right, grows in the middle of the world, spanning the earth and the sky, the finite and the infinite, the mortals and the gods. In vegetal life, everything begins from the middle, as we will see in chapter 1, which is a beginning that dwells on the question of the beginning, demonstrating the speculative identity of *genesis* and *phytogenesis*. The strange inversions we will sample there will continue in chapter 2 dedicated to the vegetal weirdness of being in time, where Aristotle and Hegel, among others, will be prompted to usher us to the roots and seeds of time. Awaiting the reader on the other side of the pivotal chapter are extended meditations on two features of time as a plant: diachrony and anachrony. With the help of sexual difference (chapter 4) and spectrality (chapter 5), respectively, we will gauge the contrapuntal rhythms of diverse temporalities and the disjointedness of their modalities. Both features, it will be argued, constitute time by de-constituting its identity in an unmistakably vegetal key.

Probably the most famous philosophical figuration of time as a plant (the time of spirit captured in thought, the time of philosophy, no less) appears on the pages of the preface to Hegel's *Phenomenology of Spirit*, where the dialectical and "progressive unfolding of truth" takes its cues from vegetal metamorphoses: "The bud disappears in the bursting-forth of the blossom, and one might say that the former is refuted by the latter; similarly, when the fruit appears, the blossom is shown up in its turn as a false manifestation of the plant, and the fruit now emerges as the truth instead. These forms are not just distinguished from one another, they also supplant one another as mutually incompatible. Yet at the same time their fluid nature [*ihre flüssige Natur*] makes them the moments of an organic unity in which they not only do not conflict, but in which each is as necessary as the other."[8]

---

7 Mircea Eliade, *Patterns in Comparative Religion*, translated by Rosemary Sheed (London & New York: Sheed & Ward, 1958), p. 269.

8 G.W.F. Hegel, *Hegel's Phenomenology of Spirit*, translated by A.V. Miller (Oxford & New York: Oxford University Press, 1977), p. 2.

One of the premises behind *Time Is a Plant* is that it is necessary to make time for time, that is, to take the time for thought and imagination to delve into or to glide on time's dynamics and to revel in its stasis. In a haste to impose teleological reason onto the development of philosophy (and, with it, of spirit— hence, of all that is), Hegel does not make time for time. While resorting to the allegory of vegetal metamorphoses, he does not linger either with time or with plants. By lingering *with Hegel*, in what follows we will attempt anachronistically to correct his oversight.

Formally, the assertion that time is a plant may be reminiscent of Hegel's half-ironic remark in the *Phenomenology* that "the being of spirit is a bone [*das Sein des Geistes ein Knochen ist*]."[9] The ironic bit in the dialectical statement is the truth it teases out of phrenology, showing that even a pseudoscience that relates the shape of the skull to a person's character holds a grain of truth. The sense of Hegel's remark is speculative: it establishes the dialectical identity of opposites, of externality and interiority, appearance and essence, the shape of a bone and personality traits, but it remains absurd when taken at face value, when the identification of the extremes with one another is immediate. For its part, "time is a plant" is a thesis at once speculative and literal, not to be dismissed as a metaphoric or allegorical expression of abstract subject matter.

To do justice to plants and to time is to account for the coincidence of teleology and a-teleology, completion and openness, fruition and non-fruition. Time comes into its own *and* is irrevocably exilic. Its identity is a non-identity: when it is most "in itself," it is in exile, diasporic, dispersed. A plant, too, is at home in the other, in self-externalization, the maximization of its exposure with all the dangers and good omens inherent in this condition. Lashed by rain and gusts of wind, many cherry blossoms will fall to the ground without metamorphosing into cherries. Buds will not give way to flowers if bitten by unexpected morning frost. Oranges will not mature as they would otherwise after a sudden hailstorm batters them. The fall, failure to open or to launch, and non-maturation are also their time, along with the completion, devoid of a final accomplishment, of the reproductive process, which need not be sexual. Time is fruition and non-fruition, the ripe moment and an utterly contingent occurrence.

Our adventures in the vegetality of time are just beginning ... as always in the middle,

in medias res ...

---

9 Hegel, *Hegel's Phenomenology of Spirit*, p. 208.

CHAPTER 1

In the Beginning: On Phytogenesis

The beginning does not begin as it should. Least of all, when we begin with the beginning, in and at the beginning, for instance, with the canonical *In the beginning, God created heavens and earth.* To begin with, there is either too much or too little there, in the beginning. Or, indeed, both: too-much-too-little.

The tired theological question *Did God create the world out of nothing—ex nihilo—or out of something?* concentrates in itself the religious as much as the secular paradox of the beginning, of a *genesis* invariably nullified by itself. If the world is created out of nothing, then the beginning is also nil: it does not exist, for, as soon as there is something, it is no longer a beginning. If, conversely, the world is created out of something, then the beginning will have been preceded by something else that will have begun before it, again denying it the honor of being a beginning. In secular (or, at least, in secularized) terms, the beginning detained at a unique and clearly identifiable point in time is not a beginning but a stop-frame reality. Suffice it to press the *play* button, and the beginning evanesces, now as a mere transitional moment in the temporal flow.

The incipient Biblical words themselves, *In the beginning ...*, begin with a major confusion, which translations from Hebrew to Greek and on to English and other languages only aggravate. *Bereshith* (בְּרֵאשִׁית) is rendered in the Septuagint as *en archē* (Ἐν ἀρχῇ).[1] Lost in translation is the signification of the Hebrew word, meaning "in or at the head." One does not begin abstractly with the beginning; rather, what first emerges (as in the birth process) is a figure, or a figuration, of that which claims to be the first. Namely, a head. Or a shoot. We ought to put to one side the can of worms this interpretation opens: In whose head did God create heavens and earth? His own? Or, do heavens and earth stand for the double head of creation itself? What matters for our purposes is that the Greek *archē*, the complexities of which Latinate derivations try to express with recourse to the couple *principle/principal* (the first Biblical verse in the *Vulgata* reads, *In principio creavit Deus caelum et terram*), takes over the beginning, disembodying, if not decapitating, it. And this is not to mention the absence of *genesis* in *Gen.* 1:1, that other word for the beginning, lending the inaugural book of the Pentateuch its Greek title.

---

1   In the translation of *Gen.* 1:1 by Aquila of Synope, the first words are rendered in Greek as Ἐν κεφαλαίῳ, referring literally to the head.

© MICHAEL MARDER, 2024 | DOI:10.1163/9789004679894_003

Whatever happens or fails to happen at that point in the beginning erases the beginning. In Greek—and not only—*Genesis* entitles the translation of the book that in Hebrew is known as *Bereshith*, but, instead of *genesis*, we find *archē* among the book's opening words. (Nor is the "original" safe from the inner displacement of the origin: the first letter of the Hebrew text is not the first in alphabetical order, *aleph*, but the second, *beth*). So, what if we were to perform the opposite hermeneutical-exegetical gesture, insinuating *genesis* in place of *archē*, and, thereby, rendering the beginning anarchic?

Here, a brief overview of the significations of *genesis* in ancient Greek is in order. With this word, Plato designates birth or being born, as in *Phaedo* 88a— *prin kai genesthai hēmas*, "before we were even born." Then, in *The Republic*, he reads becoming into *genesis*, advising against studying it and advocating, instead, a contemplation of being, of what neither arises nor perishes: "If [a study] compels you to contemplate being, it is suitable, if becoming— unsuitable [*ei de genesin, ou prosēkei*]" (526e). Aristotle distinguishes between absolute becoming, as coming-into-being, and relative becoming, as becom-ing-this-or-that: "for we say that he who learns becomes learned [*gignesthai men epistēmona*], but not that he comes to be as such [*gignesthai d'haplos*]" (*De Gen. et Corr.* 318a35).

These and many other texts interweave the two semantic threads of *genesis*: (1) coming to be and (2) continuing to become. *Genesis* is the source or the ori-gin *and* that which emanates from the origin, the event and its repercussions, the instant and a chain of instants arranged in a succession, a point and a line. *Genesis* is the origin of time, and it is, itself, in time. One cannot unsnarl this conceptual knot without undercutting the intelligibility of what is tied in it.[2] Articulated as *genesis*, the beginning does not have an end, insofar as it spreads to everything and everyone springing forth from it. Nor does it have a begin-ning, because there is no definitive cut preceding it, no void, but birthing from the other. (Even in *ex nihilo*, the preposition *ex*—out of—emphasizes the con-tinuity of emanation, despite the radicality of derivation from the void, from nothing.) Further still, in its sense of birth or birthing, the genetic beginning, *genesis qua* beginning, involves the whole of nature, which, in Latin, is tied to the verb *nascere* (to be born) and its past participle *nato* (born). Whether as

---

2 Derrida ascribes this double sense to, at once, a "formal" and a "naïve" approach: "genesis, when it is examined naively and in the most formal way possible, brings together two con-tradictory meanings in its concept: one of origin, one of becoming" [Jacques Derrida, *The Problem of Genesis in Husserl's Philosophy*, translated by Marian Hobson (Chicago & London: The University of Chicago Press, 2003), p. XXI]. Yet, this formal naiveté, itself a contradiction in terms, will shadow the concept throughout.

coming to be or as continuing to become, the beginning is tied to birth, even when it touches upon cultural, cultured, or self-cultivating activities, such as learning (as in the Aristotelian "becoming learned").

Births, however, vary immensely—from the hatching and parturition of animals to the germination and budding of plants. In the light of these differences, *genesis* appears to be much more vegetal than *archē*. The dimming down of clear-cut beginnings and ends, in the midst of an account given of the beginning, focuses on the ever-extending metamorphosing middle, closer to a germinating seed than to an emerging head. The extension of this middle in the generative process also sketches out a vegetal manner of being born, retaining the organs that tether the existent *in statu nascendi* to the earth, instead of cutting the umbilical cord. And, despite differences between animal and vegetal births, plants are representative of all beings, comprehended in the indelible words of the *Bhagavad Gita* as the manifestations of the middle: "Beings are such that their beginnings are unmanifest, / Their middles are manifest [*vyakta*], / And their ends are unmanifest again. / What complaint can there be over this?" (11.28).[3]

More than that, plants are rooted both in the earth and in the sky, which are the two worlds, the two elemental milieus, they inhabit simultaneously (a simultaneity, a *simul*, that holds the key to the spatial interpretation of time), coming closer, in their singular fashion, to the universality of what was in the beginning, from the very beginning, riven in two—the sky and the earth. They thrive in the middle between the two extremes that start making sense as the extremes that they are thanks to the dynamic vegetal position. I would thus like to venture my first hypothesis, borne out in incomparable ways by each new beginning: *all genesis is a phytogenesis, whether or not plants are present in or expressly absent from its unraveling.*

• • •

Although it sounds equivalent to the composites "anthropogenic" or "technogenic," "phytogenic" is substantively distinct. The other adjectives are essentially causal attributions, imputing responsibility for this or that occurrence to human beings or to technology. "Phytogenic" may have a causal tinge, as well, but it bears on the ontological plane much more than its ostensible analogues. *Genesis* describes the ongoing activity and behavior of plants toward themselves and toward a livable world. In light of their enviable capacity for

---

3   *The Bhagavad Gītā*, 25th Anniversary Edition, translated by Winthrop Sargeant, edited by Christopher Key Chapple (Albany, NY: SUNY Press, 2009), p. 113.

regeneration and self-refashioning, losing and adding on organs according to the seasons and environmental circumstances, plants are the virtuosos of *genesis*; in the middle of existence, they start each time from the beginning of themselves and of the world. In the continuity of their lives, they keep returning to and reviving the discontinuity of the instant.

In a decidedly human context, the capacity to begin repeatedly is, for Hannah Arendt, first, the event of being born and, second, the capacity to act, where the beginning "is not the beginning of something out of something but of somebody, who is a beginner himself."[4] Her word for the first beginning as our phenomenal appearance in the world is *natality*, recapturing *via* Latin *nātus* (born, arisen), aspects of the Greek *genesis*. The sheer fact of the plurality of such beginnings, of humans understood in the first place as *natals* rather than *mortals*, is a countervailing force vis-à-vis the totality and all tendencies toward totalization. The real standoff, then, is that of *genesis* and time—*genesis* as time imbued with, on the one hand, a radically separate, discontinuous, and absolute instant and, on the other, continuous emanation—against the totality and the tyranny of pure space.

The second beginning, according to Arendt, germinates in our self-recreation together with others through speech and a shared action that is properly political (but also vegetal).[5] I am sure that plants were not on Arendt's mind when she formulated her theory of political action as the second beginning, the other natality, a new *genesis*. But, following her own criteria, plants are the perpetual beginners, who recommence over and over again, thanks to their inventive self-articulations and communicative interactions with other plants, with fungi and bacteria in the soil, or with insects and other animals above the ground. In this, they are also consummately political, reborn together others ...

Inspired by a heterodox reading of Arendt, my second hypothesis is that *to be a plant is to be a beginner*, or, in other words, that there is a secret equivalence between the two parts of the composite word *phytogenesis*. *Phyto = genesis*. After all, the verb, from which the Greek for plant (*phuton*, which also means "tree," "child" or "descendant," and "creature") and for nature (*phusis*) derive, is *phuein*—to grow, as much as to emerge, to beget, to be born, and, hence, to begin, to come-to-be.[6] (I should mention, within a parenthesis which could

---

4   Hannah Arendt, *The Human Condition*, Second Edition (Chicago & London: The University of Chicago Press, 1998), p. 177.

5   Arendt, *The Human Condition*, p. 9. For more on the vegetal and phoenix-like "second birth" in Arendt, see the final chapter in my *The Phoenix Complex: A Philosophy of Nature* (Cambridge, MA: The MIT Press, 2023).

6   C.S. Lewis, *Studies in Words*, 2nd Edition (Cambridge, UK: Cambridge University Press, 2013), p. 34.

be extended almost indefinitely, that our contemporary negation of nature as a meaningful concept is, in the first and last instances, a refusal to continue speaking and thinking in Latin, to keep abiding by everything the translation or mistranslation of *phusis* into *natura* has implied over centuries. "Without nature" entails nothing more and nothing less than "without 'nature'." All too often, and unbeknownst to themselves, such negative and dismissive gestures end up affirming a patchwork of elements that inhere in *phusis*. Delatinizing "nature," what conceptual and natural language or languages do those making such gestures choose to speak?).

In the word itself, as this word, *genesis* will have been preceded: it rebegins what *phyto-* has already announced and begun otherwise. In the same breath, *phytogenesis* says the first and the second beginning, the two folded into one and each unfolding both in itself and in the other, in the middle, between the other and itself. Redoubled, the beginning (or the instant) is bolstered and displaced or disordered, stays put and is set in motion: energized. It emerges from the density of the elemental abode, is born, comes to be and grows without giving up on the freshness of its inception, faithful to its roots and punctuating the continuity of linear emanations, turned back into the points (*puncta*) that they are. This is the time of the beginning and the beginning of time in time, transcendence in the immanence of being.

My first and second hypotheses—like the first and second beginnings, like *phyto-genesis* itself—convey the reversibility of the subject and the predicate. They say, in effect: every beginning is a plant and every plant is a beginner. The two halves of the statement are implicit in St. Hildegard of Bingen's quasi-concept *viriditas* ("the greening green"), with which she designated the self-refreshing capacity of finite existence in general and the self-recommencing life of plants in particular.[7] We should proceed with caution, however, seeing that this phytogenetic beginning is not an origin; it is not at all inconsistent with being in the middle and with commencing always in and from the middle of actual existence. If, together with plant (*phuton*), nature (*phusis*) names a beginning—as in Empedocles' Fragment 8: "there is neither a *phusis* nor an end of all mortal things"[8]—, then meta-physics attempts to break, once and for all, with the already constituted beginning, and to position itself after, as much as behind, that beginning as the true origin and end of all things. Every project of *prima philosophia* (of "first philosophy": fundamental, constituting and itself un-constituted) is stamped with this anti-vegetal and anti-temporal desire of metaphysics.

---

7   For more on this, see my *Green Mass: The Ecological Theology of St. Hildegard of Bingen* (Stanford: Stanford University Press, 2021).

8   Lewis, *Studies in Words*, p. 34.

In contrast to the origin, which is but a head cut from the rest of the body, the beginning does not stay enclosed in itself, immune to external changes and inner transformations. As soon as it is, it bursts forth into generation, a moving lineage in an ongoing tension with the starting point. A beginning, or a rebeginning, configured as nature-plant (*phusis-phuton*) grows, decays and metamorphoses, refuses a definitive end in ending, indefinitely returns (perhaps: and this *perhaps* is more and more uncertain in the twenty-first century) after the end. An origin, conversely, clings to the illusion of its unperturbed immutability.

The beginning proper to plants is beginnings, corresponding to the two milieus they inhabit at the same time and everything proliferating between them. This "at the same time" actually illuminates multiple temporalities of vegetal existence, their anarchic beginnings without beginning below and above ground-level, their rootedness in all elements—it was Empedocles, once again, who deemed all four elements to be roots, *riza*[9]—and the elements' rootedness in the activities of plants. Two become four, and four strive to infinity, if, as Aristotle has it, "the plant possesses potential root and stock [*echei kai rizan kai kaulon dunamei*] in every part" (*Parva naturalia* 467a23–24). Another splitting of a fictitious, unified and coherent origin takes place here and is infinitely repeated within the boundaries of vegetal finitude. Its repetition is the work of time.

Living in two different environments at once, plants track the movements and time of celestial bodies, while also staying in touch with the subtler time of subterranean transformations, of decay, of micro-organismic communities making it possible. These temporalities are the mutually complementary facets of becoming: metamorphosis in the light and metabolism in the dark obscurity of the soil. Experienced astronomers and geologists, plants not only passively track these times, but also actively—inter-actively, within the framework of individual-collective plant behavior, and inter-passively, by contributing a bulk of their own mass to planetary metabolisms—constitute them. In this regard, we might say with a greater degree of precision: *In the beginning, plant created the sky and the earth.*

• • •

In a more restricted, scientific sense, *phytogenesis* means (1) the growth and development of a plant, often at a cellular level, and (2) the emergence and

---

9   "Hear first the four roots of all things [*panton rizomata proton*]: shining Zeus, life-bringing Hera, Aidoneus and Nestis who with her tears fills the springs of mortal men with water" [Fr.6, Empedocles, "Fragments." In G.S. Kirk & J.E. Raven, *The Presocratic Philosophers: A Critical History with a Selection of Texts* (Cambridge: Cambridge University Press, 1963), p. 323].

evolutionary development of plants. The notion rehashes the basic ambiguity of *genesis*, its vacillation between a radical cut and a continuation, a new commencement and ongoing development, transcendence and immanence. All the while, it remains dynamically suspended between rapidly multiplying bivalent meanings.

Besides, *phytogenic* signifies "caused by or consisting of plants," as in *phytogenic dam, phytogenic dune*,[10] and *phytogenic shores*, "formed as a result of the life activities of plant organisms."[11] The conflation of various scales and levels of existence and analysis is not accidental here, either. The same composite word of Greek provenance describes the development of a single plant, of plant communities molding landscapes and waterscapes, of a species and of the entire biological kingdom with their heterogeneous histories. It puts plants in the position of the objects of evolutionary, geological, biological, ecological, cytological, and other kinds of study *and* acknowledges their role as subjects in crafting themselves and their worlds.[12] Correlatively, phytogenic processes are handed over to objective time measurements—those pertaining to the deep time of evolution; the ecosystems' water, carbon, and nitrogen cycles; or mitotic development—*and* they figure in the constitution of subjective time, expressed at the level of molecular memory and its retrieval or potentiation of the lifeworld, replete with orientations toward what is above and what is below a living being in its milieu. Phytogenesis thus reveals how plants are in time *and* how they are zero points, from which time radiates ever anew.

The scientific use of the term goes back to Matthias Jacob Schleiden and his 1838 essay "*Beiträge zur Phytogenesis* [Contributions to Phytogenesis]," where the concern is with cell origination, division and renewal. There, phytogenesis comprehends the microscopic and the macroscopic planes of vegetal existence, in that "every plant, developed to a somewhat higher degree, is an aggregate of fully individualized independent beings, even the very cells." "Each cell," Schleiden continues, "leads a double life: an entirely independent

---

10   "Phytogenic," in *Academic Press Dictionary of Science and Technology*, edited by Christopher G. Morris (San Diego & New York: Academic Press, 1992), p. 1644.

11   "Phytogenic shores," Igor S. Zonn et al. *The Caspian Sea Encyclopedia* (Berlin: Springer, 2010), p. 331.

12   With regard to the imbrication of geological and phytological time, refer to the work of German late-nineteenth-century botanist Otto Kuntze, who coined the term "phytogeogenesis." [Otto Kuntze, *Phytogeogenesis: Die Vorweltliche Entwickelung der Erdkruste und der Pflanzen* (Leipzig: Verlag von Paul Frohberg, 1884].

one, belonging to its own development alone; and an incidental one, in so far as it has become the constituent part of a plant."[13]

Schleiden is equally preoccupied with the question of plant development and origination, both of them implied in phytogenesis. The doubling he attributes to the life of the cell cannot but affect its origin, which, split into two, is indefinitely displaced, transposed onto the terrain of multiple beginnings, originally temporalized—and, hence, ceases being a "pure" origin. Further, the mechanism of cell renewal, which he discovers with the help of state-of-the-art microscopes using Zeiss lenses, is, itself, a doubling, the replication of chromosomes and their subsequent separation into two daughter nuclei in the process now known as mitosis.[14] In the course of phytogenesis, the physical division of the nucleus (and subsequently of the cell) is everywhere shadowed by the metaphysical division of the origin against itself, shattering in the same stroke the illusions of metaphysics. All this transpires *genetically*, in, at, and as the beginning that is a continuation and a continuation that is a new discrete beginning.

Schleiden relies on experimental methodology in his studies of plants as a counterpoint to speculative botany, spearheaded by Goethe and Hegel. But this does not prevent him from reaching conclusions that are analogous to theirs. Regardless of the method they follow, Schleiden and the philosophically motivated botanists chance upon the speculative identity of a part and the whole. For Goethe, this identity hinges on the leaf—at once a part of plants and a generic-genetic principle, on the basis of which all other plant parts are formed.[15] What is original here is the superadded and the superfluous, namely the leaf that, as a leaf, is seasonally shed and regrows and that, as other organs into which it metamorphoses, keeps growing and decaying. Not only does Goethe de-essentialize the vegetal origin, stripped of its identity and revealed as secondary in its supplementary function, but he also de-linearizes time itself, putting in question its successions and sequences: as in the deconstructive logic of the supplement, the second comes first, and the first second. Phytogenesis, on this view, is not the productive generation, germination, and teleological development of plants. Nor is it reproductive cyclicality, tied to the seed. Rather, it makes itself obscurely felt in the play of a leaf, in the ongoing

---

13   M.J. Schleiden, "Contributions to Our Knowledge of Phytogenesis." In *Scientific Memoirs, Selected from the Transactions of Foreign Academies of Science and Learned Societies*, edited by Richard Taylor. Volume 2 (edited by Richard Taylor (London: Richard & John Taylor, 1841), p. 281.

14   Schleiden, "Contributions," pp. 283ff.

15   Johann Wolfgang Goethe, *The Metamorphosis of Plants* (Cambridge, MA: The MIT Press, 2009), p. 65.

experimentation with the leaf's thickening and rarefication, extensions and contractions, reception of solar energy, emission of oxygen in photosynthesis, and carbon release in decay. The time of vegetation and the vegetality of time hinge upon such playful conflations, volatile changes of positions, reversals, twists and turns beyond the logic of productive and reproductive economies.

On the experimental side of things, Schleiden calls the organelles of plant cells that capture his attention *cytoblasts*: "As I have to treat of an entirely peculiar, and, as it appears to me, of a universal elementary organ of vegetables, I do not deem it necessary to excuse myself for applying to this body a definite name, and shall term it Cytoblast (χῦτος βλαστός) with reference to its function."[16] The "universal elementary organ of vegetables" echoes Goethe's quest for the *Urpflanze*, the original plant or plant archetype, condensed in the original organ, the leaf. Schleiden attends to an organelle, the organ of a cell, that houses phytogenesis in its productive or reproductive sense. At first blush, the organelles that appear under his microscope lens seem to be the antipodes of leaves; they are those segments of cells, including above all the nucleus, where development takes place. The Greek *blastos* refers to a germ, or a bud, from the verb *blastanein*: to bud, to sprout, to grow. But, just as leaves are, for Goethe, the unstable units of metamorphosis, so cytoblasts are the sites of vegetal excess, inflecting the present with the future. The vessels of sprouting and growth, cytoblasts are the containers of the uncontainable, of what, by definition, overflows their limits. They encapsulate the growing beings and the perpetual beginners that plants are, effecting the speculative identity of vegetal parts and the whole, of the instant and branching, convoluted, knotted chronologies.

From plant cells, the theory of phytogenesis was applied to animal cells at the hands of Schleiden's colleague Theodor Schwann, who came to believe that all animal structures were made up of cells. "Schwann believed the genesis of cells was similar to crystallization, with cells freely forming an intercellular fluid. Despite Schwann's orthodox Catholic conservatism, he was quite content to explain the formation of the fundamental units of life by a mechanical process that appeared to be something like spontaneous generation."[17] The incipient ambiguity of genesis and, within its genre, of phytogenesis seeps into its application to animal life: mechanicity and spontaneity, rigid crystallization and free fluidification, the past and the future become interchangeable. But what is noteworthy is that phytogenesis does not stay limited to the emergence and development of a plant or of plants; it involves living beings without formal

---

16   Schleiden, "Contributions," p. 283.

17   Robert J. Richards, *The Tragic Sense of Life: Ernst Haeckel and the Struggle over Evolutionary Thought* (Chicago & London: The University of Chicago Press, 2008), p. 130.

membership in the kingdom *Plantae*, as well. This is a matter of ontological necessity, rather than that of historical contingency, whereby the structure and the process were first discovered in plants, only to be subsequently rediscovered in animals. The discontinuous and continuous character of time makes itself uniquely felt in the ruptured and uninterrupted relation between plants and animals, spanned by phytogenesis, the relation that remains unrepresented in the phylogenetic tree (itself, a vegetal image) of life's branching continuities.

Schleiden's theoretical opponent Hegel eyes all beginnings with suspicion, including those of organicity and life with respect to plants. In Hegel's system, the beginning is the most abstract, least determined state that, having been posited, has not yet undergone enough negations to attain dialectical concreteness and self-differentiation. Plants are not an exception to the rule of the dialectical critique of beginnings: "the vegetable world" is "the first stage of being-for-self, of reflection-into-self: but only immediate, formal being-for-self, not yet the genuine infinity."[18]

Phytogenesis, in keeping with the philosophy of Hegel (who does not, however, resort to this composite word), is the inception of organic existence glimpsed through the prism of the concept, a "reflection-into-self" that begins to round off the circle of subjectivity. This rounding-off in plant life, the return of a living vegetal being back to itself, is still incomplete, the bending of its itinerary not yet sealed at a point where the beginning and the end meet. Thus, instead of a "genuine infinity" of self-reflection in a circular relation, plants embody in the stages of their growth the "bad infinity" of a straight line. "Plant-life therefore begins where the vital principle gathers itself into a point and this point sustains and produces itself, repels itself, and produces new points."[19] Isn't this, though, an apt description of time, of the "principle" of time that, gathered into an instant, both sustains and repels itself, falling apart into a multiplicity of instants? The beginning of plant life, as Hegel sees it (or, in our terms, phytogenesis), is the paradoxical beginning of time.

Implicit in Hegel's account is the supposition that the abstraction of geometrical elements appropriately represents vegetal existence because, like basic geometry, vegetality makes a bare, abstract beginning—of spatiality and understanding in the one case, and of life in the other.[20] The negative

---

18   G.W.F. Hegel, *Philosophy of Nature: Encyclopedia of the Philosophical Sciences, Part II*, translated by A.V. Miller (Oxford: Oxford University Press, 2004), p. 303.

19   Hegel, *Philosophy of Nature*, p. 303.

20   Space and understanding, too, are no more than the beginnings of dialectical mechanics and the phenomenology of spirit at the stage of consciousness devoid of self-consciousness, respectively.

self-relation of a point produces a line, which consists of an infinite number of such points; the point of plant life, representing "the vital principle," is a seed that repels itself by way of physical elongation and ramification in growth, later on culminating in new seeds. Needless to say, the explanation is faulty, as is, also, every attempt to describe the point of the beginning, the beginning as a simple atomic point. Already in the thickets of Hegel's text, the self-gathering of the vital principle betrays a previous dispersion it must overcome for plant life to commence. Analogously, in the dialectical mechanics of Hegel's philosophy of nature, the point is not the origin; it is produced, rather, through the self-negation of an infinite and indeterminate space. The seed is a product of past plant life, not a starting point, or, more accurately, it is a starting point and an end point simultaneously, much closer to the good infinity of a circle than Hegel likes to think. The instant is a punctuation mark and a point of intersection of various sequences that precede and succeed it.[21]

As organic figures of "the vital principle [that] gathers itself into a point," seeds are beginnings without beginning and ends without end. As we shall see, not only is the sexual reproduction of plants a counterphase of vegetative growth and not only does it negate, if we are to believe Hegel, the vegetal mode of being and mark a dialectical transition to animality, but it also devolves back to geologic nature: "In the seed and the fruit the plant has produced two organic beings [zwei organische Wesen] which, however, are indifferent to each other and fall apart. The power which gives birth to the seed becomes the earth [die Erde]; it is not the fruit that is the womb."[22] The principle of phytogenesis is both posterior and anterior to plants. How can this mélange of the *after* and the *before* gather itself into a point? In what ways can the two "indifferent to each other" become one, who or that is also two, but, precisely, non-indifferent inasmuch as reflected into themselves (or into itself)?

Inadvertently, Hegel got something right about phytogenesis, in which the origin is divided against itself, genetically. It is now prudent to add that this "itself," against which the origin is divided, is unequal to itself on the two sides of the equation. Rather than a simple self-alienation of *genesis* that, having departed from its static purity and given rise to differentiated development,

---

21   In *Grafts: Writings on Plants* [(Minneapolis: University of Minnesota Press, 2016)], I explored this structure of the instant with regard to the vegetality of time in the works of Clarice Lispector: "The instant is, at once, fruit and seed, the end and a new beginning. Living is juicing the instant in an effort to get to its promising seed, which will germinate into another one, and another... In no way does this 'extraction' involve violence perpetrated against the world nor against anything in it. Since the instants weave the fabric of who I am, the juicing of the fruit is the juicing of myself" (p. 133).

22   Hegel, *Philosophy of Nature*, p. 349.

anticipates its future self-reconciliation, the division of and at the origin involves *genesis* and *phyto*, the two that, while they seem to say the same thing semantically, are radically different from (and, perhaps, indifferent to) one another. *Phyto* = *genesis*, but the opposite, obviously, holds as well: *phyto* ≠ *genesis*. Any further contributions on phytogenesis will do well to take the conjunction of these two formulas into account.

• • •

Phytogenesis is, to fall back on phenomenological discourse, a "worldly genesis,"[23] empirically verifiable and constituted by something or someone else, even as it is also, to a certain degree, constitutive. Taken in this sense, phyto- or worldly genesis is an imperfect genesis, one that is neither transcendental nor pure nor absolute, that is to say, absolutely free of—uncontaminated by—already constituted elements. Nonetheless, a pivotal argument in Derrida's 1953–54 dissertation on *The Problem of Genesis in Husserl's Philosophy* is that there is no such thing as a pure, unconstituted, or strictly transcendental genesis at all; if anything, genesis implies "essential rootedness in the continuity of being, in time, in the world" or "a wavering once more between *a priori* ideas [...] and a simply 'worldly' genesis."[24] "Essential rootedness" immediately coexists in the logic of genesis with uprootedness, a non-inclusion or an inclusion that is not total within its milieu. Similarly, with respect to time: "the creative or 'radical' aspect of genesis would disperse it in an infinite multiplicity of absolute beginnings that are neither temporal nor atemporal nor historical nor suprahistorical."[25]

According to the criteria Derrida elaborated in his dissertation on Husserl, all genesis is worldly, with empirical and transcendental components braided so that no analysis, no analytical exercise, is able to set them apart. The genesis of conscious intentionality arises from the synthetic unity of sense, of unelaborated experience, of preunderstanding. The genesis of time is "disperse[d] [...] in an infinite multiplicity of absolute beginnings." Phytogenesis sees, in turn, the emergence of plant cells from a preexisting cell before it undergoes mitosis, and, in line with its other significations, entails the stimulation of vegetal growth by the past metabolized in organic decay and the many offshoots of evolutionary development (Darwin's "origin" of species) from prior species

23   Derrida, *The Problem of Genesis*, pp. XLI, 3.
24   Derrida, *The Problem of Genesis*, pp. XXXII, 3.
25   Derrida, *The Problem of Genesis*, p. XXXII.

(Darwin, in fact, postulated that a process analogous to mitosis writ large may be responsible for the emergence of new species[26]).

The moment of genesis is that of coming to appearance, a distinctly phenomenological theme. Hence, Derrida: "the theme of the historico-intentional genesis, the theories of 'sedimentation' and of 'reactivation' (*Reaktivierung*) presented in the *Origin of Geometry* would only make explicit the dialectic of 'protention' and of 'retention' described in the lectures on 'internal time consciousness.' The genesis would be an unveiling."[27] The instant, registered in the present, would then be an instant of disclosure, of appearing in the open and on the horizon of time consciousness. This opening and this horizon are, however, enveloped by the hidden, by what has receded into the no longer retained past and what has not emerged from the future beyond protention. Underlying genesis as "an unveiling" is the time of the obscure, of the unapparent out of which every coming to appearance is potentiated *along with* internal time consciousness. Derrida's Husserl acknowledges a "deeper temporality" that runs along these lines, only to shirk back from it and dissolve it in timelessness.[28]

Assuming that genesis is or would be an unveiling, the time before or after time is the gestation that precedes the moment of birth. In plants, the coming to appearance is manifestly and vitally incomplete: their roots stay hidden even as their aboveground organs seek maximal exposure. Phytogenesis is a veiled unveiling, the time of gestation continuing in tandem with the time of birth, of an ongoing birthing. But human existence, too, is a mutated version of phytogenesis: while we do not have any physical parts of ourselves buried in the earth (during our lifetime), the interiority of the body and of the mind belongs to the obscure background of the unveiling, as does the unconscious, or, in a phenomenological key, unthematized infra-experience, lived outside or underneath the meshwork of intentionality. We are, in a certain sense, buried in ourselves—as other to ourselves within ourselves—and we germinate out of our being buried in ourselves, ever so incompletely emerging into the light, starting over again and again. Is that another genesis or the other of genesis? Another time or the other of time, where the future beyond protention merges with the past before retention?

As far as Husserl himself is concerned, "primordial genesis" is responsible for the formation of time consciousness. It is a passive synthesis of the three

---

26   Charles Darwin, *The Origin of Species and the Descent of Man* (New York: Random House, 1957), pp. 89ff.

27   Derrida, *The Problem of Genesis*, p. XXXIII.

28   "Husserl nevertheless ends by reducing temporality to an eidetic structure that has already been constituted by an originarity that is atemporal" (Derrida, *The Problem of Genesis*, p. 5).

modalities of time, translated into retentions, presentations "connected to any kind of intuition," and protentions. "The rubric, protention, designates the second aspect of genetic primordial lawfulness that strictly governs the life of consciousness as the time-constituting unitary stream. Just as a retentional horizon of the past is invariably connected to each impressional present, a protentional horizon of the future is no less invariably connected to an impressional present. Just as one can disclose the retentional horizon, so too can one expose the protentional horizon."[29] Rather than a one-directional teleological orientation toward the future, time consciousness comprehended as "primordial genesis" is a vegetal emanation from the middle, from "an impressional present" and its corresponding intuitions, retaining past impressions and anticipating the future ones. The basic -tention of retention and protention, which is also at the heart of intention, is as much spatial as it is temporal, as much an intending as an extending, shared by human consciousness and plant growth. That is the genesis of "primordial genesis."

In addition to linking the three modalities of time into a "unitary stream" of time consciousness in the subject, primordial genesis is also charged with the task of unearthing the history of the object: "Another 'constitutive' phenomenology, the phenomenology of genesis, follows the history, the necessary history of this objectivation and thereby the history of the object itself as the object of possible knowledge. The primordial history of objects leads back to hyletic objects and to the immanent ones in general, that is, to the genesis of them in original time consciousness."[30] The subjective aspect of time consciousness is but one half of the whole it makes up together with the "history of the object itself" in genetic phenomenology. Yet, both the subjective and the objective facets of genesis are reflected in the phenomenological unity of time consciousness and object history, itself traceable back to "original time consciousness," without which no historical sense is possible. In the same way, as the adjective *phytogenic* intimates, the world-creating capacity of plants is the common denominator of the subjective and objective dimensions of phytogenesis.

Phenomenological genesis is not governed by questions of substantive order or priority, the very questions that usually come to an impasse around the-chicken-or-the-egg conundrum. Bracketing the issues of substance and causality, the phenomenological investigations do their utmost to describe the order of appearance in and for conscious apperception. The rose of consciousness is

---

29   Edmund Husserl, *Analyses Concerning Passive and Active Synthesis: Lectures on Transcendental Logic*, translated by Anthony Steinbock (Dordrecht: Kluwer, 2001), p. 115.

30   Husserl, *Analyses Concerning Passive and Active Synthesis*, p. 634.

without a "why." Apropos of this, Husserl writes: "Let us note throughout that these intuitive memories do not, for instance, come first in genesis; instead, the corresponding empty presentations are essentially earlier."[31] Empty presentations are the beginning *from the standpoint of conscious experience and the phenomenology of time consciousness themselves*; later on, they are "filled" when their ties to the corresponding intuitions surface.[32] The "intuitional" underside of their retentional and protentional moments comes after and finds its rightful place in the environmental or perceptual horizons, which are, Husserl insists, constitutive,[33] in an analogous manner, in which the environmental context is constitutive for plant growth. An abstract mode of thinking is bogged down in empty presentations, including abstract views of time (that have, in the meantime, acquired a sense of immediacy) with discrete instants cut off from one another. Genetic phenomenology demonstrates that the empty continuum of time comes first and that it may remain free of the intuitions that would fill it precisely by connecting it to retentional and protentional horizons. Turning to vegetal extensive intentionality and, specifically, to the vegetality of time is a reminder to take an extra step of identifying the environmental and perceptual horizons of time.

Primordial genesis does not, despite the gist of this expression, belong to the past; to locate genesis in a coming to appearance, as Husserl does, is to detach it from the singular event of animal birth and to entrust it to the ever-burgeoning vegetal birthing, of consciousness as much as of *phusis-natura*. The vegetality of time is a replay of genesis (as a phytogenesis) located in presentations and in the perpetually crumbling and self-recomposing present. In other words, genesis is always happening; it is the very happening of every happening, of every event of appearing in the light, ensconced in the sheltering darkness. In this vein, Husserl writes: "the rubric 'association' characterizes for us a form and a lawful regularity of immanent genesis that constantly belongs to consciousness in general" and emphasizes, once again, "the lawful regularity of genesis prevailing in subjective life."[34] The immanence of genesis, its constant accompaniment of consciousness from within, is vegetal birthing, of time as much as of consciousness, of time consciousness and its associative connections. In the

---

31   Husserl, *Analyses Concerning Passive and Active Synthesis*, p. 117.

32   In this sense, Hegel's phenomenology of spirit and Husserl's phenomenology of time consciousness are implicitly in agreement with one another.

33   "If we now consider the genetically more original modes of making co-present, then at issue, e.g., for every perceptual object, are its entire horizons that are constitutive of it, horizons that belong immediately to it" (Husserl, *Analyses Concerning Passive and Active Synthesis*, p. 117).

34   Husserl, *Analyses Concerning Passive and Active Synthesis*, pp. 162, 163.

same gesture, Husserl de-absolutizes genesis, here and throughout his work, by inserting it in chains of associative connections, by not letting it persist in a state of separation as an absolute beginning unaffected by everything that follows it. His view of genesis—hence, of consciousness and of time—is wholly vegetal.[35]

The vegetality of the phenomenological genesis is not limited to the subject or to subjective life alone; it inheres in the phenomenon itself. In association, "the one points to the other—even though there is still not an actual relation of indication by signs and designations. Further, the phenomenon gives itself as a genesis, with the one term as awakening, the other as awakened. The reproduction of the latter gives itself as aroused through the awakening."[36] Phenomena in their appearing that is essentially superficial—that fashions the essence out of the surface of appearances—are also essentially vegetal. In chains of association that are both spatial and temporal, they play the role of proto-signs and of points of genesis with regard to other phenomena they tacitly evoke, refer to, or associate with.

The present and the presentations that first strike the eye are *presentiating*, bringing to appearance and into co-presence the other phenomena they associatively awaken. But this movement, as temporalizing, need not take place actually, in actuality. It is in connection with the apparent futility of something appearing or said futilely, without enduring, for nothing *and* in connection with the opposite of an "abiding value" that Husserl invokes vegetal processes: "I can by reflecting make observations and can make completely useless assertions, *none* of which have even the slightest tinge of enduring truth; they only have the barren, fleeting relevance bearing *on* the fleeting life *of* the present. Yes, actually barren, for fecundity is precisely something of abiding value and not something merely existing in a moment of growth."[37] The vegetality of time is both—actuality and possibility, fragility and tenacity, the non-enduring, merely existing life of the present expressed in growth and the abiding value of fecund potentiality.

---

35 Remarkably, Husserl writes of subjectivity that it "is indeed only conceivable in genesis" (*Analyses Concerning Passive and Active Synthesis*, p. 171).

36 Husserl, *Analyses Concerning Passive and Active Synthesis*, p. 166.

37 Husserl, *Analyses Concerning Passive and Active Synthesis*, p. 452.

CHAPTER 2

The Vegetal Weirdness of Being in Time

FIGURE 1   Gustav Klimt, *Die Erfüllung* ("Fulfillment"), 1905–1909
PHOTO: © MUSEUM OF APPLIED ARTS, VIENNA (MAK)/
GEORG MAYER

The two are locked in a mutual embrace, her head slanted and resting on his shoulder. The woman's eyes are closed; her face rapt, she appears ecstatic. The one she embraces towers over her, kissing the side of her neck (unless, in a vampire move, he is sucking her blood) and supporting her swooning head with the left arm wrapped around and behind her. The woman's own arm threads its way underneath and through the embrace, all but meeting her other hand. Her fulfillment is on display, shining through the position of her head and facial expression. It is there for everyone to see, even as she, herself, sees nothing; that of the lover remains a mystery.

There is, however, something weird about the scene—not least because it strives to evince weirdness itself with all the swirling branches in the background and serpentine shapes rolled in the foregrounded robe of the figure, who turns away from the viewers. An alternative title of this frieze from the Stoclet Palace in Brussels, currently in the collection of the Museum of the Applied Arts (MAK) in Vienna, is *Die Umarmung*, "The Embrace." Fulfillment, as the play of titles suggests, is to be sought in the fullness of the embrace. Upon a closer look, nonetheless, the circle made of the woman's arms is, like plant subjectivity according to Hegel, imperfect; open, it leaves a gap, through which a piece of the man's robe shows. There is no direct correspondence between the fullness of fulfillment and the rounding of the embrace. Things are more complex than that. Fulfillment is to be found not in the other, but in the embrace of the other, that is to say, in the embrace of the embrace, a coimplication of imperfectly closed, fragile circles on the verge of falling apart.

Besides the eyes incrusted at the center of the spirals that adorn the back of the robe (the eyes that, along with those growing on the tree in the background, watch the viewer), the weirdness of the scene oozes from the mediation of the immediate that is the embrace. Putting my arms around the other, I miss the other, seeing that the circle the two arms create is incomplete. At best, I embrace the embrace of the other, echoing the words and deeds of *The Song of Songs*, "Let him kiss me with a kiss of his mouth" (1:2).[1] Weirdness lurks in the

---

1 Interpreting these words in *Sermons on the Song of Songs*, Bernard of Clairvaux says: "The mouth that kisses signifies the Word who assumes human nature; the nature assumed receives the kiss; the kiss, however, that takes its being both from the giver and the receiver, is a person that is formed by both, 'the one mediator between God and mankind, himself a man, Christ Jesus'" (II.3). In turn, as though kissing and embracing St. Bernard's words, St. Hildegard of Bingen writes: "But let the one who sees with watchful eyes and hears with attentive ears welcome with an embracing kiss my mystical words, emanating from me, the living one [*Sed qui vigilatibus oculis videt et attentis auribus audit, hic mysticis verbis meis osculum amplexionis praebeat quae de me vivente emanant*]" (*Scivias* II.7 [*Hildegardis Scivias*, edited by A. Führkötter. Corpus Christianorum Continuatio Mediaevalis, Vol. 43

twirls and undulations of mediation, the perforated fold of the middle where
the two embraces or kisses meet, multiplying two by two (two arms, two lips
on each side), and, further still, by an infinity stretching between them despite
physical approximation.

In my interpretation of the Klimt piece, I want to follow in the footsteps of
St. Bernard of Clairvaux, who saw in the Biblical "kiss of his mouth" an allegory of Christ who was the point of intersection, at which divine nature kissed
human nature. So, rather than a human lover embracing a woman (or embracing her embrace), I suggest that it is time that holds her in its arms. This time
is no doubt weird, because it appears as a figure, with a human-looking shape,
which also verges on the dissolution of a figure. Anonymous, faceless, reveal-
ing its face only to the embracing and embraced woman who seems not to
notice it in her rapture, this figure of time *befits* her—her, whose time it is. The
embrace is a silent confirmation of that fit.

That said, the fittingness of the embracing and the embraced is, itself,
unfitting, inapposite, inappropriate. The interlinking of two imperfect circles,
of arms that are open in wrapping around the one whom or that which they
embrace, fails to encase her, him, or it. Holding and held fast by the time made
exactly to their measure, human beings exist in such a way that, whenever
they are on time, they are either too early or too late—above all, for themselves. There is no such thing as *on time* in matters of existence, which is essentially untimely, fittingly unfitting. Any sense of fulfillment issuing from time's
embrace must contend with its essential untimeliness.

Loving and intimate as it may be, my relation to the time that is mine (befitting, rather than appropriated by, me; the time, in which I am enveloped, no
longer distinguishing myself from it) is going to be a largely unconscious affair.
Eyes closed, standing over and against but not facing her lover, the woman in
Klimt's *Die Erfüllung* could have been already dead, were it not for her right
arm that inches up to complete the embrace, resisting the force of gravity.
While ecstatically surrendering herself, she embraces the embrace, sustaining
it with an affirmation as superfluous as it is necessary. What does it feel like to
be *in* it, in time's embrace?

I may be running a little ahead of myself; who cares, if I am always too early
or too late (for myself)? I would write, in a sort of shorthand, that to be in time's
embrace is to be. To embrace its embrace is to become. But this does not yet
convey the sense of abiding in the embrace of time. From Klimt, we have an
indication, *via negativa,* of what this abode does *not* feel like. In the intimacy

---

(Turnhout: Brepols, 1978), henceforth referred to as 'CCCM 43']; PL 197: 564d). And, of course,
it is a divine kiss that will be betrayed with Judas' perfidious kiss.

of the embrace, our eyes are closed; we touch and are touched without seeing. Since we are in the arms of time, which is also between our arms, this not-seeing is neither foreseeing nor glancing back. "In" time, we see neither the future nor the past, because there is nothing to be seen, nothing available for vision there. We get in touch with the past and the future otherwise—for example, through touch, the contact afforded by an embrace and the embracing of the embrace. Swathed in the pleated fabric of time, we are finally enwrapped in ourselves, if without facing ourselves, without staring at a mirror image of ourselves, without the dialectical safety nets of self-recognition in the other. The condition of such envelopment in oneself is not narcissism, and the act of embracing time's embrace is not fatalism; it is freedom.

Being in time is, thus, lingering in the arms of time, in its embrace, which, for all that, does not detain the one enduring or perduring there (for the time being). We slip through time's arms and hands, just as it slips through ours. This transient being-in is, equally, a being-between—in an embrace, between two arms multiplied by the other two and by countless wrinkles and pleats in the fabrics that cloak them. It is, to be precise, being-in-between, the meantime or the meanwhile, in which everything whiles away.

The distance that the *between* wedges into the tightness of the embrace makes seeing possible. The organs of that decidedly strange vision have already come into our view: the eyes painted on the back of the robe and those, stylized as the ancient Egyptian "eye of Horus," growing on the tree in place of fruit. Memory and anticipation, the past, the future, and their respective visions are externalized and delegated to vegetal and animal natures (the robe is bedecked with birds, some of whom might be further allusions to Horus, traditionally depicted with the head of a falcon). Behind the woman locked in and embracing time's embrace, a tree watches her; ahead of her, eyes, surrounded by spiraling ellipses and belonging to various birds, stare from the robe of her lover. Everything is back-to-front here: the figuration of time is with its back to the future—the only plausible anticipatory vision; the woman, in turn, stands with her back to the past, anonymously invigilated by a tree. Trying to get in touch with what is to come, she can do no more than touch the eyes, with which the robe is festooned, with the palms of her hands resting on it. And, if she were to do so, if she were to touch—blindly, intuitively—the eyes on the back of time, she would cover them, too, preventing their own seeing.

What the twirls of tree branches, the spirals around painted eyes, the interlinked albeit half-open embraces, and the title *Die Erfüllung* variously demonstrate is that time is not a straight arrow flying from the past through the present to the future. Assuming that time admits a geometric representation (which betrays its more intimate relation to space than such abstractions

would allow), its passage will be curved, zigzagging, bending and twisting into
weird shapes. Its bends, waves, convex or concave surfaces, parabolas and
ellipses, hyperbolas and circles will be neither purely contingent nor predetermined. They will plot the contours of time's embrace, both uniquely fitting and
absolutely indifferent to each embraced thing. I will henceforth find myself in
the arms of time, between the hands of a sublime clock set in motion just for
me and shared by all that is.[2]

• • •

When, as we have glimpsed in the preface, Einstein twisted Galileo's and Newton's theories out of their habitual shape, which had cast a shadow over the
science of physics for centuries, he revealed the twisted nature of space and
time, or, more accurately, of spacetime. (In the word itself, as this composite word, time embraces and is embraced by space.) Defining gravity as the
curvature of spacetime,[3] Einstein implied that curving does not befall time
and space *a posteriori*; that their homogeneity and abstract undifferentiation
are no more than useful fictions spread by classical physics; that warping is,
therefore, constitutive of spacetime. In our terms, gravity is the spatiotemporal
embrace of a thing. By what?—you may ask. By the warping effect of its own
dynamic force field. As physicist John Wheeler famously formulated this relation: "mass grips spacetime, telling it how to curve; spacetime grips mass telling it how to move."[4] That is why the embrace of time, which is inseparable
from that of space, both befits each thing, determined by and determining it,
and is radically unfitting around the open edges of its warpage.

Between poetic and colloquial discourse, we might say that a day is measured by the sun's embrace of the horizon, its span extending from east to west
in a celestial curve that hugs the curving line of the earth. This way of thinking
or speaking equates a day to the period of daylight, while leaving the nocturnal
part out. A day, nonetheless, encompasses daytime and nighttime; it embraces
the shining and the obscure, what is most proper to it and what it is not, the

---

2 Isn't it quite odd that in our epoch of a nearly dogmatic critique of "linearity," the most vocal
   of such critiques embrace the "flatness" of, say, "flat ontologies"? The mismatch of basic
   geometric and trigonometric imaginations is yet to be analyzed.

3 "Gravity is special. In the context of general relativity, we ascribe this specialness to the fact
   that the dynamical field giving rise to gravitation is the metric tensor describing the curvature of spacetime itself, rather than some additional field propagating through spacetime;
   this was Einstein's profound insight" [Sean Carroll, *Spacetime and Geometry: An Introduction
   to General Relativity* (Cambridge: Cambridge University Press, 2019), p. 48].

4 Quoted in Tom Siegfried, *Strange Matters: Undiscovered Ideas at the Frontiers of Space and
   Time* (Washington, DC: Joseph Henry Press, 2002), p. 141.

fitting and the unfitting. The same goes for life, or a lifetime, which is among the senses of *day*. A life entails also what it is not, itself and its other: death. Living is nourishing oneself on and communing with death in the embrace of existence. As always, plants excel in literalizing this insight.

The tightest embrace is, of course, that of a black hole. The warping of spacetime in a black hole is such that it does not let anything, not even light, escape past the line of the "event horizon." The fit of the embracing and the embraced is absolute: the circle is shut closed, fulfillment complete. The trapping power of the black hole is described as a tornado-like "whirling drag" in the direction of singularity,[5] absorbing all meaning and sense without emitting any. In this whirling curvature of space, time slows down, and, taken together, these two tendencies amount to the warpage of spacetime that feeds on itself: "The hole's space is warped by the enormous energy of its warpage. Warpage begets warpage in a *nonlinear* self-bootstrapping manner that is a fundamental feature of Einstein's general relativity laws."[6] The circularity of the embrace may be sensed in the self-referentiality and self-propagation of warpage, its energy that seems to require no other to grow.

The singularity, toward which the whirling drag tends, is analogous to death—and not only because a black hole is born from a massive dying star. Dying is moving in spiraling circles, or along less predictable trajectories, toward the singularity of death. Once one crosses the event horizon, no meaning will bounce back, even though the dense meaninglessness of singularity orders and organizes the rest of existence behind one's back. Time slows down for a consciousness approaching the moment of death in the whirling curvature of life's space: from the standpoint of that consciousness, that moment never arrives, just as from the vantage point of someone who has already crossed the event horizon, the line of the horizon appears to be still ahead. The embrace of time in death chisels out the edges of finite existence, but it does so not as the Grim Reaper, who comes for the dying one. Heidegger and Levinas were both right and utterly wrong: individuating and deindividuating, the most singular and the most implacably general, death is the embrace of oneself by oneself as (already) other to oneself.

In relativity theory, spacetime curvature defined by gravity forms a sort of transition zone between the mass of a thing that conditions the curve and the curve that regulates the movement of the thing. That is to say, spacetime is

---

5 Kip Thorne, "Warping Spacetime," in *The Future of Theoretical Physics and Cosmology: Celebrating Stephen Hawking's 60th Birthday*, edited by G.W. Gibbons et al. (Cambridge: Cambridge University Press, 2003), p. 79.

6 Thorne, "Warping Spacetime," p. 78.

neither internal nor external to the thing that exerts its gravitational pull. Only in special relativity, which, reflected in Newtonian mechanics, is the theory of spacetime in the absence of gravity (and, therefore, in the absence of curvature) are things, time, and space separated from one another. So, what is the sense of being "in time," when spacetime puts in question the difference between being inside and being outside?

Here is a dry scientific response: "Spacetime is a four-dimensional set, with elements labelled by three dimensions of space and one of time. An individual point in spacetime is called an event."[7] Yet, these are definitions heavily biased toward space, its dimensions, points, and so on. We have no other choice but to raise the question anew, without, however, discarding the spatialization of time so long as it is concurrent with the temporalization of space. And, as we raise it anew, we might lean on something quite old: the thinking of time in ancient Greece.

• • •

Whatever happens, takes place in time. What kind of place? What does *in time* mean? Is time indifferent or minutely adjusted to "whatever happens" in it? How can a spatial preposition apply to a temporal development? And does this strange interiority, presumably devoid of extension, imply the existence of an exteriority, where, perhaps, nothing happens?

These questions, resonating with the one I have just raised with regard to the spacetime of relativity, are vast, so much so that they may accommodate, embrace, welcome in their disquietude an entire tradition of philosophy extending from Aristotle to Hegel, Bergson, and Husserl, the tradition Heidegger criticized in a famous footnote in *Being and Time* and Derrida revisited in an essay pretending to be no more than a note on that footnote.[8] While he was eager to admit that the essence of technology was nothing technological, Heidegger could never accept a parallel thesis that the essence of time was

---

7   Sean Carroll, *Spacetime and Geometry: An Introduction to General Relativity* (Harlow: PearsonEducation, 2014), p. 4.
8   Jacques Derrida's essay in question is titled "*Ousia* and *Grammē*: Note on a Note from *Being and Time*," in *Margins of Philosophy*, translated by Alan Bass (Chicago & London: University of Chicago Press, 1982), pp. 29–67. Heidegger's note is included at the very end of the book, in a section on "Within-timeness and the genesis of the ordinary conception of time." Marked as note xxx. in the English translation of *Being and Time* by Macquarrie and Robinson, it aligns Aristotle's and Hegel's respective prioritization of the *now* in the thinking of time and argues that the model for the comprehension of time is essentially spatial (New York: Harper & Row Publishers, 1962), p. 500.

nothing temporal. For him, a geometrical conception of time boiled down to a baneful philosophical misconception, a vulgar everyday understanding that modeled within-timeness (*Innerzeitigkeit*) on the spatial sense of being-in.[9] The entire argumentative thrust of his magnum opus was an attempt to formulate an existential notion of time and its corollary, inwardness purged of any and all reminders of space.

Heidegger claims exclusive guardianship over time irreducible to spatial figures and numeric quotients. I want to show, however, that the impurity of time Heidegger rejects is vegetal and that the structure of existence he calls *ecstatic* is weird time, twisting and turning into the opposite of a pure conception. In what follows, Aristotle will be my guide, notably the dense pages of Book IV of *Physics*, which Heidegger skimmed over and all too quickly dismissed. This, to be sure, will be neither the Aristotle of the Western tradition nor that of Heidegger himself. Simply put, I propose to retrieve the weirdness of Aristotle in order to reactivate the weirdness of "being in time."

Etymologically speaking, weirdness is a becoming that winds on, bending, turning, and, detour upon detour, turning *into* something else.[10] It absorbs the inward and the outward, while rendering both wayward. And, at the same time, it signifies fate or destiny, a destination that is impossible to reach as intended, if only because every intention perverts itself all by itself: "And out of wo into wele / Youre wyrdes shul chaunge."[11] Weird time consists in twists and turns that turn things into their opposites: woes into good fortunes, growth into decay, the same into the other, the extended into the intended, and (why not?) space into time. To be in time is to perdure in the twisting and turning, to dwell nowhere but in the swerve, the curve that, by dislodging entities from their fixed places and identities, gives them an opportunity to happen, to take place, to be welcomed in the moment said to be opportune, ripe, properly theirs. It is to experience a dislodging that dispenses to each their own and, conversely (this *vers*, too, is a turn of the weird), an ownness that brings to naught, that destroys and makes fritter away (*katatēkei o chronos* [*Physics* IV.XII.221a33]).[12]

---

9 Heidegger, *Being and Time*, p. 338 (except for pages including the editors' footnotes, all numbers refer to the pagination of the book's German edition).

10 "Weird." *An Etymological Dictionary of the English Language*, edited by Walter W. Skeat (Oxford: Clarendon Press, 1888), p. 702. The centerpiece of the etymology of "weird" is the Proto-Indo-European root **wer-*. The Latin *vertere*, to become, derives from the same root.

11 Thomas Wright, *The Vision and the Creed of Piers Ploughman* (*with notes and a glossary*), Volume 2 (London: John Russell Smith, 1856), p. 540.

12 Aristotle, *Physics, Books* I–IV, translated by P.H. Wicksteed and F.M. Cornford. Loeb Classical Library, Vol. 228 (Cambridge, MA: Harvard University Press, 1932). All references to this text will follow the standard Greek pagination. Often, translations are mine.

How to interpret this tenuous ownness granted to everything by its time? Observing the world of plants, we stumble upon the idea of seasonality (an appropriate period of the year for sowing and harvesting; of fruit that is in season or out of season) and extend this idea, in line with the melancholy wisdom of the Hebrew *Kohelet* (*Ecclesiastes*), to all existence: "There is a time [*z'man*] for everything and a season [*'et*] for every activity under the heavens: a season [*'et*] to be born and a season [*'et*] to die, a season to plant and a season to uproot [...]" (*Eccl.* 3:1–2). Modernity, in turn, is subtly defined by living out of season—a condition, in which it espies the humanity of the human—, by untimeliness, say, that of Nietzsche's meditations (*Unzeitgemäße Betrachtungen*).

But Aristotle says something else altogether, and it is worth listening carefully to the strangeness of his words without normalizing them by means of a "commonsense" translation or a conviction that his conception of time is ordinary.[13] As he considers being "in time," *en chronō* (*Physics* IV.XII.221a19), Aristotle concludes that "all the things that are in time are embraced by time [*ta en chronō onta periechesthai hupo chronou*], just as with other kinds of being-in; for instance, things that are in places are embraced by place" (*Physics* IV.XII.221a28–30). Time is the most intimate of embraces, virtually inseparable from each thing it embraces. Prior to the distinction between passive and active voices, it is a twisting, a turning, a bending, rounding off, including, encompassing (*periechein*) that which is in it. It sets up a perimeter around each thing that keeps to that very thing's shifting outlines. Rather than a firmly held possession, the thing that is in time's embrace is let go of, or, better, it is held *in such a manner that* the holding itself lets it go, sends it to meet its destiny in weird circles, the detours that outline the curving or the rounding of time.

Here, Aristotle goes further than *Kohelet*. Among the lines of that Biblical text, we find: "a time to embrace and a time to maintain distance [*'et lekhabok v'et lerakhok*]" (3:5). A rhythmic alternation of opposites (here: embracing and distancing) is disrupted by the Aristotelian notion of time itself as an embrace. For, what is "a time to maintain distance" in the context of time that embraces the embrace as much as the distance? The quasi-seasonal timeliness of actions appropriate to a situation at hand, on which the Biblical author insists, stands in contrast to the untimeliness of time. Or, rather, it stands in contrast to another regime of timeliness, more singularly attuned in its embrace of everything, even of distancing.

The embracing of what is in time by time seems to be a tautological expression repeating the same word, if preceded by a different preposition. The circle

---

13   The latter is Heidegger's take on Aristotle's notion of time in Book IV of *Physics*.

drawn by repetition is another instantiation of time's weirdness: it performs (repeats), right in the body of a philosophical text, the operations of time with its welcoming embrace, as open to receiving as to parting with what it receives. Repeating is doubling and doubling over that which is repeated. It is a strategy of weirding. The welcoming embrace of time is also doubled (unless it doubles) that of a place, which similarly embraces whatever and whomever is in a place. And time counts begin, at minimum, with 2 (for instance, two *nows*), with doubles that, by virtue of a gap between them, diverge from one another despite their identity. "There appears to be no time between two 'nows' when we fail to distinguish between them" (*Physics* IV.XI.218b30). All time is a mean-time, a between-time (*metaxu chronos*) that unfurls and presses on from the doubled to a doubling different enough for someone to discern the difference.

・・・

If the two instances of *now* are akin to points in space (and Aristotle, indeed, calls them points, *stigmata* [*Physics* IV.XI.220a11]), then time is what passes—appears and disappears; appears in and as disappearing—between these points. Between them, Aristotle sketches a line (*grammē*: *Physics* IV.XI.220a16), and he is taken to task for this geometrico-philosophical gesture by Heidegger. Nonetheless, a straight line connecting two now-points would not be capable of embracing, circumscribing, welcoming anything unless it were bent, twisted, weirded. What warps it (and ultimately cuts it short) is that the *nows* are not only points but also limits admitting of a continuity that is markedly discontinuous, ruptured, punctuated. "Through the now, time is continuous [*sunecheia chronou*: time is held-with, had or held together] [...] and, as a limit of time [*peras chronou*], the now-point is at once the beginning [of the future] and the end [of the past]" (*Physics* IV.XIII.222a10–13). At once linear and non-linear, spatial and nonspatial, time is itself and its other (that is, space). Since its identity stems from a perpetual casting off of fixed identities, it is well suited for embracing all that is with a liberating embrace, not detaining but releasing what is in time to its destiny, to its own weirdness.

Time is weird space without extension, the space that is twisted and twisting out of spatiality through an array of spatial figures: points, limits, lines, turns, curves. That is the gist of Hegel's notion of time as the self-negation of space, its *Aufhebung* that, in a twisted way, cancels out and preserves spatiality.[14] Inspired by Aristotle, he writes in *Philosophy of Nature*: "Negativity, as point, relates to space, in which it develops its determinations as line and

---

14   In this sense, Hegel's conception of time is anything but ordinary, the charge Heidegger levels against it alongside his critique of Aristotle: "No detailed discussion is needed to

plane; but, in the sphere of self-externality, negativity is equally *for itself* and so are its determinations; but, at the same time, these are posited in the sphere of self-externality, and negativity, in so doing, appears as indifferent to the inert side-by-sidedness of space. Negativity, thus posited for itself [*an sich selbst Negative*], is time."[15]

A chain of negations concretizes spatial existence: a determinate point negates the indeterminacy of space; the reflection of one point in another from which it is different and in which it is still recognizable negates the point and produces a line; the self-negation of a line is a plane, and so on. Space expresses "motionless coexistence," because it is given all at once (*háma*), held or had together in *sunecheia*, as Aristotle would have said. Time, on the contrary, is movement, notably the movement of negativity, which traverses and unhinges the perfect unity of space. It is not a later addition to spatial reality (how to measure this belatedness outside of time, not *in* it?), but is there all along in the determinate negations of space, puncturing and punctuating continuous and contiguous relations.[16] Time is the in-between of transitions from abstract spatiality to a point to a line to a plane, in the course of which space grows more richly differentiated and concrete. Perspective matters: to have a foretaste of time, instead of focusing on those things between which transitions happen, we need to look at the in-between, where or when the happening of the transition negates that from which and that toward which it transitions. This happening *is* time, "negativity, thus posited for itself."

Time, then, is weird or weirded space, but the movement of *Aufhebung* is no less weird; it is dialectical weirdness par excellence, the twisting and turning, the destructive-generative perversion of a beginning. One trait of their shared weirdness is the ruptured continuity and the continued rupture of becoming, which Aristotle transposes onto a lapse between two *nows*: "Whenever we recognize that there has been a lapse of time, by that act we recognize that something has been going on [*alla mēn kai hotan ge chronos dokē gegonenai*]" (*Physics* IV.XI.219a7–8). We become aware of the passage of time when we take note of the fact that we have not taken note, that inexorable and ongoing changes have escaped our attention. In other words, our inner chronometers (*chronos metron* [(*Physics* IV.XII.221a1)]) are set off when we concentrate on a

---

make plain that in Hegel's interpretation of time he is moving wholly in the direction of the way time is ordinarily understood" (Heidegger, *Being and Time*, p. 431).

15   Hegel, *Philosophy of Nature*, pp. 33–34.

16   In an addition to the paragraph from *Philosophy of Nature* where he defines time, Hegel writes: "In pictorial thought, space and time are taken to be quite separate: we have space and *also* time; philosophy fights against this 'also'" (p. 34). In this sense, time is there "all along" despite its emergence from the negation of space in dialectical logic.

lacuna between the two now-points we are comparing, that is, on "negativity posited for itself," as Hegel has it, not on the seamless plenitude of one and the same *now*.

The time of vegetal growth (and of decay) illuminates this character of time as such. The increase or decrease of a plant's extension may be observed only across an interval of not attending to it, a gap, in which something has been imperceptibly going on. Time-lapse photography reveals the movements of plants, because it plays with the lapses, the intervals of vegetal events, to which our perceptual apparatus is unable to attend "in real time."

At the level of the concept, too, the negation of space within space and its negation *tout court* converge, making time weird. For Hegel, "the point, the being-for-self, is consequently rather the *negation* of space, a negation, which is posited in space."[17] It is a determination in space that occupies no space. Time is also a negation of space that preserves, concretizes, and elevates what it negates, albeit as "negativity posited for itself." It shares with the point not only the activity of negating space but also the quality of being-for-self, and this makes the point (as a *now*) weirdly spatiotemporal, spanning space and time. Difference *in* space morphs into difference *from* space. As soon as the abstract indifference and nondifferentiation of space are negated, being in space becomes indistinguishable from being in time.

The very language of time is borrowed either from the science of space or from that of numbers. Hegel is adamant about this: "There is no *science of time* corresponding to the *science of space*, to *geometry* [...]. The differences of time have not this *indifference* of self-externality which constitutes the immediate determinateness of space, and they are consequently not capable of being expressed, like space, in configurations. The principle of time is only capable of being so expressed when understanding has paralyzed it and reduced its negativity to a *unit*. This inert One [...] can be used to form external combinations, and these, the numbers of *arithmetic*, can in turn be brought by the understanding under the categories of equality and inequality, of identity and difference."[18]

Spatial figures and arithmetic express nothing other than a certain understanding of time, one that has paralyzed temporal flux, congealing it in lines or numbers, and that has reduced the negativity of a transition (or what we have earlier designated as "between-time") to a measurable (countable) unit. But the problem goes deeper than identifying an erroneous understanding of time, which could be corrected by another mode of understanding. Given the place

---

17   Hegel, *Philosophy of Nature*, p. 29.
18   Hegel, *Philosophy of Nature*, pp. 37–38.

of understanding in Hegel's *Phenomenology*, it would stand to reason that time is better appreciated by what comes dialectically after this stage of consciousness, namely self-consciousness. To understand time is, thus, to fail to understand it with the static schemes and molds at the disposal of this faculty.

So, what does self-consciousness bring to the table that is absent from mere consciousness? Self-consciousness is the torsion or the twisting of consciousness that attends to itself at the same time that it attends to the outside world. Its doubling, its distribution between itself and the other, a repetition that occurs simultaneously with what is repeated, is indicative of the between-time that flourishes in and as self-consciousness. The "at the same time" of self-conscious hyperattention torn between the object *consciousness* and an external object is, therefore, time itself.

Besides a shift to self-consciousness, another possibility—and one strongly supported by the spirit and the letter of Hegel's text—is that time expressed in spatial terms is inauthentic, but that it is an inauthenticity without an authentic flipside. Dialectically, nothing can be understood through itself; everything is to be conceptualized through a negation of itself. In its first determinateness (as a point), space is "the *negation* of space itself."[19] In its final determinateness (as time), space is again the negation of space itself, if no longer belonging strictly within the ambit of space. Simply put, to express time in spatial categories is to betray it in two senses of betrayal, letting it show itself and breaking the trust.

• • •

The ambiguity of time supplements its weirdness, taken as a turning or a bending. "Both its continuity and its dividedness are due to the *now*" (*Physics* IV.XII.220a5); it "is not the same as movement (*Physics* IV.X.218b19), yet it is inseparable from movement, as a "measure of movement according to 'before' and 'after' [alternative translation: according to where it comes from and what remains, MM]" (*Physics* IV.XI.219b2–3);[20] "perpetually different [*aei heteron*]" (*Physics* IV.X.218a11), it is "everywhere the same and all at once" [*autos dē pantachou háma*]" (*Physics* IV.XII.220b6). As the in-between, time is *both and* and *neither nor* in relation to these and other opposites.

---

19   Hegel, *Philosophy of Nature*, p. 31.
20   Heidegger suggests that, in Aristotle, time "is what shows itself in [...] a making-present" by way of counting. Its domestication in the present thus neutralizes its initial weirdness: "This [Aristotelian, MM] definition may seem strange at first glance; but if one defines the existential-ontological horizon from which Aristotle has taken it, one sees that it is as 'obvious' as it at first seems strange" (*Being and Time*, p. 421).

Thanks to its weirdness and ambiguity, time is bound to stay *adēlon*: unclear, murky, invisible (*Physics* IV.X.218a33), regardless of how intensely we contemplate and analyze it. It is what elapses by lapsing between two limit-points and is accessible only in retrospect, in the rearview mirror of accomplished change or in an unavoidable delay between the two objects of self-consciousness. In spite of what Husserl believes or has to say on the subject, phenomenological time-consciousness is weirdly dialectical. If we are to experience time in the fullness of intuition, we cannot be stuck in the present of perception (not least because the present of perception itself is not stuck in the present but, plant-like, grows from the middle through retention and protention); we must, rather, circle back to a *now* that belongs to the past, an event or a process that has already happened. We become aware of time's passage when something is *no longer present in a redoubled present*, when it has twisted free from the tyranny of the *now*, between the limits that now-points set for a temporal stretch. The straight arrow of phenomenological intentionality bends in such a way that time is displayed before consciousness as what has elapsed: there in not-being-there. It is constituted, for the very first time, through a repetition, a return or a replay of the lapse. Being "in" time is being in what is not itself (in what is not identical to itself) and in what is not in itself (in what "in" itself is already outside or beside itself).

Amplifying such murkiness, as a measure of movement (*arithmos kinēseōs*), time is heterogeneous. In the preceding book (III) of *Physics*, Aristotle pinpoints four types of movement, corresponding to the categories of substance, quantity, quality, and place. Locomotion, which we conflate with movement *in toto*, pivots on placeness and implies dislocation, a passage from one place to another. The remaining kinds of motion are vegetal: substantive generation and passing away (birth or germination and death); quantitative expansion and contraction (growth and decay); and qualitative change (metamorphosis and metabolism) (*Physics* III.I.201a). Would these not be disparate measures of motion, corresponding to various temporalities? Would "being in time" not lend itself to different experiences depending on whether it is the time of generation and passing away, of growth and decay, of metamorphosis and metabolism, and, finally, of displacement?

In my weird reading of Aristotle on the weirdness of being in time, the vegetality of movements measured according to categorial types builds toward the vegetalization of time. Let us take these types one by one and ascertain their embeddedness in plant life.

The substantive emergence and dissolution of a plant concentrates the discontinuous continuity of time in a seed. "A point," Aristotle writes, "both constitutes the continuity of the line it traces and also marks the end of the line that is behind and the beginning of the line in front" (*Physics* IV.XI.220a15–17). Hegel analogizes a seed to a point ("the subjective point of life") in *Philosophy of Nature*,[21] implying that the line, which culminates in it, charts previous vegetal growth (and the fruit this growth has yielded), while "the line in front" represents the growth of the plant to come. This future growth is not assured: the seed may never germinate or it may do so after an indefinite delay. Continuous with respect to the "mother-plant," it is discontinuous in relation to a plant to-come. The seed's being in time is expressed in a suspension between these two lines or limits, where, as Aristotle's text shows, the end itself vacillates between *telos* and *eschaton*, accomplishment passing over into incompletion, the process of development and maturation potentially cut short. But this seriously complicates time counts meant to measure movement: though it is one, each point/seed (*tēs autēs stigmēs*) counts as two—as the beginning and the end, *archē kai teleutē*, even as the end splits into *telos* and *eschaton* (*Physics* IV.XI.220a13–16).

The hiatus embodied in a seed spells out a sense of intra-temporality: "the generable and the destructible [...] are necessarily in time [*phtharta kai genēta* [...] *anagkē en chronō einai*]" (*Physics* IV.XII.221b29–30). They are "embraced," *periechei*, by time (*Physics* IV.XII.222a3), which encompasses, as their innermost measure, movements that are logically opposed to one another; it welcomes the one and the other, the one in and as the other. The embrace is made possible by the interrelation of opposites, confounded *and* kept apart, compiled *and* counted in keeping with the singularity of each. The innermost measure coexists in time with a count that, commemorating a feature of space whence it sprung, is utterly indifferent to what is counted. Time is always just right, or simply just, *and* totally unjust, one-size-fits-all that is expressly unfitting.

Quantitative growth and decay seem to chart a linear increase and decrease of vegetal extension in a movement Hegel associates with the essentially incomplete "bad" infinity. This is the time we are well acquainted with in modernity: the open-endedness of progress that eschews any inherent limits. Nevertheless, Aristotle situates these vegetal movements in seasonality: "Note further that there may be movement that covers the same course over and over again; in like manner, we mark off time by the year or by spring or autumn" (*Physics* IV.XII.220b13–14). Seasonality and the annual cycle that brings the seasons together depend on a turning, a circling that joins the terrestrial time of plant growth and decay to cosmic temporality governed by the rotations of celestial bodies. The weirdness of succession in a straight line inscribed into a

---

21   Hegel, *Philosophy of Nature*, p. 303. He continues on the same page: "Plant-life therefore begins where the vital principle gathers itself into a point and this point sustains and produces itself, repels itself, and produces new points."

circle is the situation of growth and decay: these lines turn out to be the tangents of a seasonal cycle, whose circumference they graze at a point that germinates in a seed or starts decomposing back into the earth. To be embraced by time in this sense is to stand at the intersection of a circle and a straight line.

Seasonality is the appropriate time for the development of those who or that are in season. Nonetheless, being out of season is not the same as being out of time; it is *still* being in time, if not at the right, opportune moment, propitious to one's developmental course. If "out of season" twists untimeliness into time, that is because the tangent still touches the circle, only at another point, where it should not have been present. The twisting and turning of what is out into what is in reflects the weirdness of being in time.

Qualitative change is the movement of becoming, conveyed with two words: metamorphosis and metabolism. In time, the othering of the same happens together with the saming of the other, rendering these opposite tendencies mutually complementary in becoming. Time's embrace means that "movement dislodges an entity from its present state [*kinēsis existēsi to huparchon*]" (*Physics* IV.XII.221b2). The dislodgement of the origin is existence as coming-out-of-a-state and transitioning to another state, which will be equally provisory. A seedling casts off the form of the seed; a fruit—that of a flower; a seed—that of the fruit that harbored it. Lending a body to becoming in its spatial aspect, metamorphosis constitutes the plant in an exemplary way, applicable to the rest of existence. Here, the same (thing) is othered, and the pace, rhythm, cadence of its othering dictates the rules of the time arithmetic.

Whereas metamorphosis is a parade of shapes that, supplanting one another, weave the fabric of ex-istence, metabolism is a throw of whatever or whoever is in time along the vectors of ex-stasis: "Change is in its nature ecstatic [*metabolē de pasa phusei ekstatikon*]" (*Physics* IV.XIII.222b16). The protocol of metabolic change (of change viewed under the aspect of metabolism, which is irreducible to—if, again, exemplified in—the physiology of digestion and the absorption of nutrients that falls under the heading of the vegetal soul, *to threptikon*) is the transcription of the other into the same, the assimilation of the other that causes it to stand beside or outside (*ekstatikon*) "itself." Heidegger's ecstatic temporality will have been preempted by the Aristotelian *metabolē*, just as the German philosopher's notion of existence will have been anticipated by *kinēsis existēsi*, the dislodging movement of metamorphosis.

More importantly, the nature of metabolism is such that the assimilating, the assimilated, and the movement of assimilation are all metabolized into time. So, "it becomes clear [*phaneron*] that all that changes [*pasa metabolē*] and everything that moves is in time [*en chronō*]" (*Physics* IV.XIV.222b30). Being in time is teetering on the edge of nonbeing, of passing away, or of having already, at least in part, passed away, given that the emergent time-consciousness should have attended to a minimal gap between two *nows*. This ambiguous being-in ought to be rigorously distinguished from an external imposition. If time metabolizes everything, it is not a gigantic immaterial stomach or intestines that digest beings, but that through which all that changes and moves metabolizes itself. The interiority of *in time* coincides with the exposure of finite existence to its own finitude, and the deeper we delve "into" it, the sooner we surface on the other side devoid of any depth. In this sense, we may speak of the vegetality of time, the movements of plants writ large in the features and essential processes of temporality, where the inner is the outer and where surfaces are preponderate.

To return to Aristotle's text, *phaneron* (obvious, evident, clear) is a counterpart to his earlier complaint about the thinking of time as *adēlon* (murky, invisible, unclear). Yet, this newly gained clarity does little to make time itself apparent or transparent; after all, it is *that in which* the changing and the moving *are*: "*pasa metabolē kai pasa kinēsis en chronō estin*," as Aristotle reiterates (*Physics* IV.XIV.223a15), adding that "time is in the earth, and in the sea, and in the sky [*einai o chronos kai en gē kai en thalattē kai en ouranō*]" (*Physics* IV.XIV.223a17–18). A double fold, then, forms, not unlike that of gravity in relativity theory: time is *that in which* the moving and the changing are, even as it is *in* the elements of the earth, the sea, and the sky. The twin of the temporal embrace is the elemental embrace of earthly things and time by the earth, of marine things and time by the sea, of the things and time of the sky by the sky. Each embrace (the temporal and the elemental) does not only clasp and hold tight the being it embraces, but it also embraces another embrace until, amidst all the apparent obviousness, it is no longer clear where the outside and the inside are; which one is more capacious, roomier, and able to envelop the other; where (and if) immanence begins and where (and if) it ends.

And a series of embraces does not stop there. In the concluding pages of Book IV of his *Physics*, Aristotle puts his finger on an aporia—"it would be puzzling, impossible, or a non-starter [*aporēseien*]," he writes—that there would be time without a soul (*psuchē*), because time is a measure of movement and, as such, it requires someone who would be doing the measuring or the counting (XIV.223a20–25). The mutual embrace of time and the elements is embraced by the psyche; *in time* comes to mean, elliptically, *in the soul*. Although Aristotle explicitly limits this first and last embrace to the intellectual part of the soul, or the "mind soul," *psuchēs nous* (*Physics* XIV.223a25–26), a vegetal soul, too, measures time, whether by using red and far-red light "to measure the length of the night,"[22] by resorting to cryptochromes and to circadian clocks in order

---

22   Daniel Chamovitz, *What a Plant Knows: A Field Guide to the Senses* (New York: Scientific American / Farrar, Staus & Giroux, 2012), p. 20.

to regulate leaf movements and photosynthesis,[23] or by discerning the times of year.[24] Since a plant's movements need to be perfectly timed and plugged into the seasonal cycle, it is, in fact, a groundbreaking chronometer (recall Aristotle's *chronos metron*), *and that is why it is a fitting candidate for the first ensoulment.*

Viewed from the opposite angle, the arithmetic of time where 2 is the smallest possible number belongs in the soul, but—a wild proliferation of embraces and interiorizations notwithstanding—it winds up *weirdly* on the outside. The exposure of finite existence to its own finitude, which is how I have interpreted being in time, dovetails with the vegetal soul that, like time itself, thrives in and on exteriority. So, what if, rather than a soul starting to pay attention to time in a gap between now-points, it is time that germinates when a plant's *psuchē* comes along on the scene of existence? In that case, the inside-out image of temporality would be part and parcel of its indelibly vegetal heritage.

• • •

The dialectical embrace of time and space in Hegel's thought yields a place, hinging—still—on the point. Time negates the negation of space by the point, which is not thereby erased but made concrete: "In this way, the *negative* determination in space, the *exclusive* point, no longer only implicitly conforms to the notion, but is *posited* and *concrete* within itself, through the total negativity which is time; the point, as thus concrete, is *place* [Ort]."[25] The concretization of a point is not due to its plotting on the vertical and horizontal axes of a system of coordinates, in three-dimensional space, or, even, as an event in the four-dimensional set of relativity theory. It is concrete as the positing of negation and the negation of the negation, that is, as the determinate negation of space by time. In fact, the point "concrete within itself" is *already* spacetime, which only in the case of special relativity is empty, and spacetime is *already* a place (which is always the place *of* something or someone). Thus, Hegel (and Aristotle before him) verges on the insights of relativity theory, when he criticizes the "usual conception of space and time [that] takes them to be *empty* and indifferent to what fills them."[26]

A place expands in its embrace to spacetime and contracts to a point. Through it—through the place that it becomes—, a point swells to the level

23   Chamovitz, *What a Plant Knows*, p. 30.
24   Chamovitz, *What a Plant Knows*, p. 157.
25   Hegel, *Philosophy of Nature*, p. 40.
26   Hegel, *Philosophy of Nature*, p. 41.

of the universal, englobing all of space (and time, to boot): "The point exists here in its truth [*in Wahrheit*], namely as a *universal* [*als ein* Allgemeines], and for this reason it is a whole space as a totality of dimensions."[27] This concrete point encapsulates the dialectical principle, where the smallest embraces the greatest and universality is concretized in a self-negated particularity. But the counterintuitive expansion and contraction of dialectical embraces is, itself, rhythmic—a little like heartbeat. It follows that the contraction of place to a point is its expansion to "the whole of space," while its expansion to spacetime is its contraction to being-in-motion.

Hegel proceeds to define a place, alternatively and more colloquially, in terms of a "unity of here and now [*Einheit des Hier und des Itzt*]."[28] These are the spatial and temporal instantiations of a point that, insofar as they exist in a unity (*Einheit*), have been already mediated with each other, intermediated. With the energy of determinate negation, a point splits into two that are embraced in a new unity of place, which is not the same as an addition of mutually indifferent elements. The embrace does not leave what it embraced unchanged: here is and is not space; now is and is not time. Dialectical unity is an upshot of the weirding that is sublation, *Aufhebung*. The unity of place is not an exception: space and time had to become weird, bent, twisted as they were concentrated in a point that exploded into the here and the now.

The weirding of a place itself has to do with the displacement inherent to it. Just as a *now* makes temporal sense only in relation to another now-point that is, precisely, not-*now* with regard to it but *then*, so a *here* makes spatial sense in relation to another *here* (which is not-*here*, there). Plus, the perversion of time in space and of space in time immanently dislocates the place and, in a gesture of establishing speculative identity, makes it inherently mobile: "This *vanishing* and *self-generation* of space in time and of time in space, a process in which time posits itself spatially as a *place*, but in which place, too, as indifferent spatiality, is immediately posited as *temporal*: this is *motion*."[29] Before we move from place to place, the place itself moves, its embrace dynamic, shifting, accommodating the contents of this place and its other, i.e., another place.

We've noted how Aristotle wrote that "things that are in places are embraced by place," this embrace mirroring and mirrored by that of time. Furthermore, movement in place, for Aristotle, has the special vegetal tinge, which we have closely examined: growing and decaying, metamorphosing and metabolizing, germinating and coming to an end. This movement appears in light of

---

27   Hegel, *Philosophy of Nature*, p. 40.
28   Hegel, *Philosophy of Nature*, p. 40.
29   Hegel, *Philosophy of Nature*, p. 41.

different parts of an emplaced thing embracing each other: being "in a place," *en topō*, is when "a body is embraced [*periechon*] by another body," but "the parts also embrace [*periechetai*] each other," and, as such, "may be in motion" (*Physics* IV.V.212a30–5). Again: an embrace within an embrace, a place in a place, potentially moving.

The thinking of place—Aristotle intimates—is as difficult as that of time, which was murky, *adēlon*: "the place appears hard to grasp [*chalepon lēphthē-nai*]" (*Physics* IV.IV.212a7). The strains of thinking converge on the interpre-tation of being-in, whether in place or in time. Actually, there should be no problem in understanding the interiority of a place, because the preposition is, precisely, spatial. Aristotle begins with this commonsense approach, liken-ing being in a place to being in a vessel. But, he concludes, "we have as good a right to regard a place as an immovable vessel as we had to regard a vessel as a movable place" (*Physics* IV.IV.212a15–16). Instead of trying to figure out what it is, we need to consider how a place works, how it sets itself to work, energizes or brings itself to actuality.

The place derives its energy from the embrace. For Aristotle, place is "an embracing limit," *periechontos peras* (*Physics* IV.IV.212a20–21). Its energy is that of limiting and bending the limit in such a way that it would embrace whatever or whomever is in place. It is a container (or a vessel) only by virtue of this embracing limit, which is more obvious, more palpable in the case of a vessel than in any other case. What happens at the curved limit, though? First, the limit, *peras*, is transformed into *eschaton*, an end in the sense of a cut, the ter-mination of a surface (*Physics* IV.IV.212a22). Second, this transformation must occur at least twice: in the embracing and in the embraced surfaces. Third, in a place, the ends touch, one of them undergirding and the other overhanging. The relation between the place and that which is placed in it, then, transpires in an intermediate zone, recalling the in-betweenness of time.

Whereas, in time, the end bifurcated into *telos* and *eschaton*, in place, it branches out into *peras* and *eschaton*. Since the latter element (*eschaton*) is the same across the difference between time and place, we should search for what makes their respective experiences of being-in unique in the distinction between the end as *telos* and the end as *peras*, an inherent objective to be attained and a limit that drops like a sharp edge. Nevertheless, even here, the weirdness of time is apparent: the now-point is responsible for the continuity as much as the discontinuity of time, for time's linearity and a break signaled by this point's transmutation into a limit, *peras chronou*. Time reconstructed from the perspective of its discreteness, from out of its gaps and lacunae, passes into place, is spatialized and emplaced in a way that is irreducible to the geometrical elements (point, line, etc.) persisting in its midst.

The embrace of a place where the ends of surfaces touch is dynamic, growing and fizzling out with the things that are in a place: "At the same time
[*háma*] the things that are in a place change their bounds, [and] so do the
limits of a place" (*Physics* IV.IV.212a30). Places are not vacant containers for
that which is contained in them; the double embrace they stage is not indifferent to the embraced. Rather, places grow and decay, germinate and die,
metamorphose—in a word, move after a fashion—with their inhabitants.
(This anticipates the speculative identity Hegel establishes between place and
motion.) Like time, places are vegetal even if they do not host actual plants:
"all bodies [*pan sōma*] that grow and move by transfer are thereby somewhere" (*Physics* IV.V.212b7–8), but "the all [*to de pan*] is not somewhere" (*Physics* IV.V.212b15), because "there is nothing outside it to embrace [*periechei*] it"
(*Physics* IV.V.212b16–7). The edge or the end of the all does not brush against
another end or edge, which is why the logic of a place cannot set itself to work
here. Not held in any embrace, the all falls apart, precluding the existence of
universal time or place, that is to say, of a totality. But, as the weirding of a spatiotemporal horizon is negated, weirdness increases exponentially: every thing
has its place in the all that is placeless.

And so, we circle back to the beginning, where what befitted each thing was
radically unfitting around the open edges of spacetime warpage, the opening
Aristotle has stripped of all edges. Such fitting unfittingness is the destiny of all
that is, weirdness as our weird (and weirdly vegetal) fate.

CHAPTER 3

Cosmic [Tree] Time

Different cultures and historical epochs have imagined the cosmos as an immense tree. This archetypal vegetal *imago mundi* indicates that the cosmos does not persevere forever in its undisturbed monolithic self-identity; it is alive; it moves, expands and contracts, flourishes and shrivels, branches out and sheds some of its parts. The cosmic tree is, therefore, virtually indistinguishable from the tree of life. But the life of the cosmos is also distinct from the vitality of an animal organism with a more or less settled shape and determinate life span. The cosmic plant develops along heterogeneous, simultaneous, and unremitting lines of growth, decay, metamorphosis and regeneration on the hither side of the teleology of maturation, ageing, and death. Its development defines the time, or the times, of the world.

The tree figuration of the cosmos puts vegetal existence on a par with the classical elements of water, fire, earth, and air, to which vegetation is actually added as the fifth element in Jain Dharma.[1] In the *Bhagavad Gita*, the eternal *aśvattha* is a tree at once of life and of knowledge. Resembling a fig or a banyan, it is a tree that is imperishable (*avyayam*) "having its roots above and branches below, / whose leaves are the (Vedic) hymns. /" (xv.1).[2] Immediately, though, *aśvattha*'s hierarchical vertical arrangement is put in question: "Below and above [*adhaścordhvam*] its branches spread, / nourished by the qualities, with objects of the senses as sprouts; / and below its roots stretch forth / engendering action in the world of men" (xv.2). The realms above and below merge into a single domain abovebelow, *adhaścordhvam*, just as living and knowing, psychical and physical realities, sensing-thinking and acting are different parts of the same vegetal being.

Jewish mysticism treats as one and the same the tree of knowledge of good and evil and the tree of life, planted in the middle of the Garden of Eden.[3] In its unique interpretation, the centerpiece of the Medieval *Kabbalah* that is the *Book of Zohar* cuts halfway the Biblical injunction, which warns against

---

1   Sibajiban Bhattacharya, *Encyclopedia of Indian Philosophies*. Vol. 10: "Jain Philosophy." (New Delhi: American Institute of Indian Studies, 1970), p. 165.

2   All citations from the *Bhagavad Gītā* are drawn from the Sargeant translation: *The Bhagavad Gītā*, 25th Anniversary Edition, translated by Winthrop Sargeant, edited by Christopher Key Chapple (Albany, NY: SUNY Press, 2009). The title of the *Bhagavad Gītā* is abbreviated as "BG" for citation purposes.

3   The idea is that, if both are in the middle, then they occupy the same spatial position and, therefore, must be one and the same tree.

© MICHAEL MARDER, 2024 | DOI:10.1163/9789004679894_005

the original sin—"From every tree of the garden you are free to eat"—thus disrupting the semantic and hermeneutical flow between Genesis 2:16 and the following verses. Separated from the rest of the text, the prohibition morphs into a permission: "everything was permitted to him [to Adam] if eaten in one-ness [*be-yiḥudah*]" (1:35b; v. 1, p. 222).[4] Adam and Eve are forewarned not about *what* cannot be taken and appropriated from their environs, but about the *how* of the taking, namely a seizing that disrespects the unity of the taken with life and creation. Knowledge, which is the sublimation of digestion and which is already present in its material form in eating,[5] must strive toward unity (*yiḥudah*): of life as such, of life and death, of life and knowledge. Considering that the entire scheme of divine emanations (or *sefirot*) was imagined in the shape of a tree, the scale and significance of paradisiac vegetal oneness are amplified to a cosmic scale.

In the cultural corpus of southern Mesopotamia, which is also one of the backdrops for the Biblical narrative, a primordial grove, or *engurra*, has at its center the sacred *kiśkana* tree ("being most certainly the black pine of the Babylonian paradise"). "It was believed to have derived its vitalizing power from the waters of life" and was rooted in the omphalos, the navel of the earth.[6] *Kiśkana* is said to have "symbolized the cosmos, often represented as a giant tree with its roots either in the nether regions or in the sky, and its branches spread over the whole earth."[7] It is important to note the interchangeability of a smaller-scale tree at the center of the earth and of the cosmic tree that gives room to the earth, the netherworld, and the sky in its various portions and organs. Both in Babylonian mythology and in Jewish mysticism, such interchangeability operates according to the rules of a synecdoche—a part for the whole, and the whole for the part—allowing for a two-way (hence, infinite) reflection of the macro- and micro-scales of existence. Pre-Socratic Greek thought subscribes to the same idea: as we have seen, *phusis*, or nature, comprehended as the overall growth of all that is, derives from the verb *phuein*, the same verb from which the word for plant as a growing being (*phuton*) is

---

4   All citations from *Zohar* refer to *The Zohar*, Pritzker Edition (12 volumes), translated by Daniel C. Matt (Stanford: Stanford University Press, 2018). Page references are to the volumes/pages in the Pritzker edition, as well as to the conventional page numbers of *Zohar*. Transcriptions from the original Aramaic and Hebrew are mine.

5   Consider the links, in Romance languages, between "to have a flavor" or "to savor" and to "know"—*sabor* and *saber*, *saveur* and *savoir*, *sapore* and *sapere*.

6   E.O. James, *The Tree of Life: An Archaeological Study* (Leiden: Brill, 1966), p. 13.

7   Ibid.

formed.[8] The naming, as well as the thinking, of plants and nature is, therefore, synecdochic.

Yggdrasil is the enormous ash or oak tree of Norse cosmology, a tree articulating diverse worlds and words, speeches or assemblies (*things*). It is the assembly of assemblies. Thor and the rest of the gods go to councils "at Yggdrasil's ash."[9] A hinge between disparate realms, Yggdrasil mediates between what is above and what is below, between the serpent at its roots and the eagle above its branches, while providing the space and the time for the messenger-squirrel Ratatösk: "Ratatösk is the squirrel named, / which has to run / in Yggdrasil's ash; he from above / the eagle's words must carry, / and beneath to Nidhögg repeat."[10] Although time passes in and as the articulations and disarticulations of the cosmic tree, Yggdrasil itself is, unlike the Indian *aśvattha*, not eternal: "Yggdrasil's ash / hardship suffers / greater than men know of; / a hart bites it above, / and in its side it rots, / Nidhögg beneath tears it."[11] So much so that "when the final battle of Ragnarök arrives, Nidhögg will finish its gnawing and bring down Yggdrasil. Then Yggdrasil will expire in flames set by the giants."[12]

In Burmese folk-tales and in alchemical practice alike, we find the sun-and-moon tree. The Lahoo narrative of creation in Burma harkens back to the time when "there was no heaven [...] / there was no earth."[13] Once heaven and earth are created, replete with four watercourses and "the sun [that] bears the duties of day, / the moon the duties of night,"[14] the sun-and-moon tree is planted, a tree that "shines as the glory of Ghusha," a co-creator god.[15] As Carl Jung points out in his alchemical studies, the philosophical tree (*arbor philosophorum*) of the alchemists similarly yielded as its fruits and seeds sun and moon. "The sun-and-moon fruits," Jung observes, "go back to Deuteronomy 33:13, '[Blessed] of

---

8   According to the unwritten cross-cultural rules of ancient and mystical traditions, there is an infinite synecdochic reflection of the micro- and macro-levels: minuscule objects are the compressed versions of cosmic realities, whereas vast realities are the expanded forms of corresponding tiny artefacts. It was in this spirit that in book 2 of Plato's *Republic* Socrates proposes to contemplate "the same script," *ta auta grammata*, of justice written in large letters in the city, rather than in a small font in a human soul (368c–d).

9   *Edda*, 29. In *The Edda of Saemund the Learned*, translated by Benjamin Thorpe (Lapeer, MI: The Northvegr Foundation Press, 2004), p. 34.

10   *Edda*, 32 [p. 35].

11   *Edda*, 35 [p. 36].

12   --, *Storytelling: An Encyclopedia of Mythology and Folklore*, edited by Josepha Sherman. Vols. 1–3 (London & New York: Routledge, 215), p. 516.

13   Gerry Abbott and Han Khin Thant, *The Folk-Tales of Burma: An Introduction* (Leiden: Brill, 2000), p. 66.

14   Abbott & Thant, *Folk-Tales of Burma*, p. 68.

15   Ibid.

the Lord be his land [...] [for] the fruits brought forth by the sun and by the moon.'" The Vulgate translation of this verse, *de pomis fructuum solis ac lunae*, was then used as the basis for the conjecture of the sun-and-moon cosmic tree (which is also the tree of wisdom, with its double reliance on diurnal knowing and nocturnal intuition) yielding such fruits.[16]

The sun-and-moon tree has a direct bearing on cosmic time, or, better, it imbibes into itself and reconciles the contrasting poles structuring this time. Bringing together day and night, which stand also for life and death among other opposites, in its morphology, it equally accommodates in its fruits or modes of shining the alterations and alternations of daily (and nightly), monthly, and annual cycles. Cosmic rhythms are grafted onto this tree, along with the very measures of time in the fashion of an ellipse, replete with two foci but lacking a clear center.[17] When it comes to the everyday time-measuring instruments we are used to, clock hands are perfectly centered, and they journey over a given space in a given stretch of time. For its part, any plant (not just the cosmic tree) is de-centered, and it *fills* space in time, as time. Despite this difference, whether in the systematization of a clock or a calendar, orientation in time looks up to and depends upon the positions, the movements, the waxing and waning, the rising and the setting, of the two celestial bodies. The sun-and-moon tree is, thus, the most perspicuous vegetal embodiment of cosmic time.

•••

The admittedly patchy overview of cosmic trees across world cultures, with which this chapter commenced, yields a conceptual X-ray of sorts, bringing to visibility their innermost traits. It shows that cosmic trees channel
- life and/as knowledge,
- energy, and
- time.

They let what they channel through their branches, trunks, and roots swirl and circulate, mediating between the darkness below and the light above, mixing darkness with light in precise proportions that sustain finite being and knowing.

---

16   Carl Jung, *The Collected Works of C.G. Jung*, Vol. 13: "Alchemical Studies," edited by Herbert Read et al. (Princeton, NJ: Princeton University Press, 1983), p. 306.

17   On the philosophical significance of the ellipse, compared to the circle, see Jacques Derrida, *Rogues: Two Essays on Reason*, translated by Pascale-Anne Brault and Michael Naas (Stanford: Stanford University Press, 2005).

When I enumerate the three ingredients that course, sap-like, throughout the cosmic tree, it may seem as though these are independent "substances" reconciled within the tremendous vegetal body of the world. In effect, their separateness is an illusion, of the kind mentioned in *Zohar* with respect to a knowledge detached from life. Each of the three terms can and should be interpreted through the other two; for our purposes, the crucial proposition is that cosmic [tree] time (or, in keeping with the insights of contemporary physics, cosmic [tree] spacetime) is the energy and the life-knowledge coursing from its roots to the trunk, branches, *and* back. It is this circulation that flattens the world pole, the vertical dimension stretching between what is below and what is above, as the *Bhagavad Gita's* term *adhascordhvam* ("abovebelow") intimates.

Another misunderstanding may arise in connection with the notion of mediation. It may appear as though the extremes—the sky and the earth, darkness and light, life and death—are primary vis-à-vis a mediation that futilely attempts to bridge them *a posteriori*. This impression, too, is far from the truth. Not only does circulation persistently return to the middle, but it also conveys that there is nothing but the middle: that the vegetally figured or configured cosmos is but a lushly proliferating middle, an infinite array of middle edges,[18] whose dynamic bifurcations and polarizations set off and keep choreographing the dance of the extremes.[19] The articulations of Yggdrasil, the assemblies that it instigates and that it *is*, are primary, which means that the cosmic origin prominently featured in mythic narration is a non-origin; it is a fecund middle that, continuously discontinuous, keeps beginning ever anew from this very non-origin or non-beginning. The time corresponding to it is a *meantime*, the plot of *in medias res*.

Cosmic time is the time of the in-between: the sun and the moon, day and night, life and death. Ernst Cassirer relates this state to how "mythical consciousness and feeling" experience "a kind of biological time, a rhythmic ebb

---

18   On the notion of plants as comprised of middle edges, see Edward S. Casey and Michael Marder, *Plants in Place: A Phenomenology of the Vegetal* (New York: Columbia University Press, 2023).

19   I have paid close attention to this issue in my recent essay, "In the Middle: Vegetal Mediations" [In *Woven in Vegetal Fabric: On Plant Becomings*, edited by Charles Rouleau (Luxembourg: Casino Luxembourg, 2022), pp. 152–177]. There, I write: "Life (vegetal life, above all) begins axiomatically in, from, and with the middle, where distinctions are never razorsharp, where things melt into one another at their edges and the inside twists into the outside. And it ends in the middle, too. Submerged in finitude without absolute starting points and finish lines, dangling or plunging in a perpetual middle, existence comes to resemble, strangely enough, the world under the aspect of eternity" (p. 153).

and flow of life, preceding the intuition of a properly cosmic time."[20] And, by the same token, the time of the in-between is a between-times, constituted by variations of intensity, tensions and torsions, clashes and mutually reinforcing feedback loops of decay, growth, metamorphosis, and reproduction. Neither unidirectionally entropic dissipation/expansion nor energetic contraction, time is both at once—the total differential of the incalculable function that is the cosmos.[21] In other words, time is a mélange of vegetal inter-temporalities.

•••

The tree-shaped figure of the cosmos implies that cosmic time is *rooted, reversible,* and *ramified.* Its roots reach to the infinite and the unknowable, such as the first and the highest divine emanation, *ein-sof* ("without end") in *Zohar* or the middle, equally infinite, the heart of the earth in the case of Yggdrasil. The idea of rootedness in infinity, instead of eternity, or in the middle subtly insists: time is not epiphenomenal; temporal realities are not merely superficial structures overlaying the deep and immutable, atemporal, essence. If the *Bhagavad Gita* emphasizes the "eternal" nature of the *aśvattha* tree, that is because, while time flows in it and as it, there is no external temporal index, no touchstone, against which these movements may be measured.

Very often the morphology of the cosmic tree is inverted, compared to that of earthly vegetation: its roots stretch above, the branches pointing down and overhang below. So, in *Timaeus*, Plato envisions the human as a celestial plant with the roots connecting the rational principle of vitality housed in our heads to the supernal sphere of ideas.[22] I have interpreted this artefact of ancient philosophical imagination as symptomatic of the way Western metaphysics inverts the order of material reality in its perverse transvaluation of existence.[23]

---

20   "Actually," Cassirer adds, "cosmic time itself is first apprehended by myth in this peculiar biological form"—here, the form of a tree. [Ernst Cassirer, *The Philosophy of Symbolic Forms*. Volume 2: Mythical Thought, translated by Ralph Manheim (New Haven: Yale University Press, 1955), p. 109].

21   For "total differentials" see Dennis Zill and Warren Wright, *Calculus: Early Transcendentals,* Fourth Edition (London & Sudbury: Jones & Bartlett, 2011), pp. 707ff.

22   "[...] we declare that God has given to each of us, as his *daemon,* that kind of soul which is housed in the top of our body and which raises us—seeing that we are not an earthly but a heavenly plant—up from earth toward our kindred in the heaven. And herein we speak most truly; for it is by suspending our head and root from that region whence the substance of our soul first came that the divine power keeps upright our whole body." (*Timaeus* 90a-b).

23   Refer to my *Plant-Thinking* (2013) and *The Philosopher's Plant: An Intellectual Herbarium* (New York: Columbia University Press, 2014), esp. the preface and chapters 1 & 3.

As Gilbert Durand writes, however, an "upside-down tree," which is also "to be found in the Sabaean tradition, in the esoteric element of the Sephiroth, in Islam, in Dante, as well as in some Laplander, Australian and Icelandic rituals," may be indicative of global reorientations that are indebted to the vegetal figuration of the cosmos: "This unusual reversed tree, which challenges our sense of ascendant verticality, is a sign of the coexistence of the schema of cyclical reciprocity and the archetype of the tree."[24]

The reversibility of cosmic tree architecture, and, by implication, of cosmic [tree] time implies that temporal flows are reversible—that the same vectors of time tend, spatially speaking, forward and back, up and down. The beginning begins at the end and at the beginning, which re-begins as though on a rewind; the end unfurls from the beginning toward another beginning, which is not assured, except by the apparatus of faith. Even the distinction between teleology and a-teleology or utter contingency is neutralized here. Cosmic reversibility may be expressed in the event of salvific resurrection or that of rejuvenation, promising the recovery of a time and a life that, assuming their unidirectional course, should have ebbed away.[25] In its secular and religious instantiations, it lends another future to the past, the future that would have been deemed impossible within the empty continuum of time, through which now-moments irretrievably pass.

Aspects of mental life confirm the reversibility of time made evident in cross-cultural takes on the cosmic tree. If the quintessentially modern idea of progress were to be valid in psychological terms, there would have been no memory in all its manifestations: the material traces of past stimuli preserved

---

24 Gilbert Durand, *The Anthropological Structures of the Imaginary*, translated by Margaret Sankey & Judith Hatten (Brisbane: Boombana Publications, 1999), p. 332. The tree of happiness in Islamic traditions is notable in this respect: "And the Prophet said: In heaven is the tree of happiness whose root is in my dwelling place and whose branches shelter the mansions of heaven; nor is there mansion or dwelling place which holds not one of its branches" [Qtd. in Bernard Carra de Vaux, *Fragments d'eschatologie musulmane* (Brussels: Congrès scientifique international des Catholiques, 1894), p. 118].

25 Eliade pinpoints a difference between the Semitic and the Indian takes on the promise of the tree of life: "'The plant of immortality and youth,' for instance, was envisaged quite differently in India and in the Semitic world. The Semites thirsted for immortality, for immortal life; the Indians sought for the plant that would regenerate and rejuvenate them" (Eliade, *Patterns in Comparative Religion*, p. 294). Similarly, he notes: *"the notion of 'salvation' does no more than repeat and complete the notions of perpetual renovation and cosmic regeneration, of universal fecundity and of sanctity, of absolute reality and, in the final reckoning, of immortality*—all of which coexist in the symbolism of the Tree of the World" [Mircea Eliade, *Images and Symbols: Studies in Religious Symbolism*, translated by Philip Mairet (New York: Sheed & Ward, 1952), p. 163].

in the bodies of things, both animate and inanimate; the genetic and epigenetic memory of living cells; an act of conscious recollection by the human psyche; and so forth. The modern conception of time coincides with the theoretical and practical abolition of memory, with the view of the mind as a blank slate, a *tabula rasa*, and the endeavor to cut all ties to the tradition as a living repository of cultural heritages. Such is a time without roots and interconnected branches, a hollow trunk leading from nowhere to nowhere, from nowhen to nowhen.

To return to the cosmic tree: it includes not only physical but also psychical phenomena on its branches and leaves, since whoever is alive, be it a living being as immense as the cosmos, is necessarily ensouled, endowed with a psyche.[26] This inclusion is discernible, for instance, in the *aśvattha* tree (which harbors "the objects of senses" as well as the rest of the life of the mind, from which practitioners are encouraged to detach themselves on the path to *nirvana* or *mokṣa*) and in the elaborate analogies drawn by St. Hildegard of Bingen between mental faculties, plant organs, and Judeo-Christian canonical figures.[27] If memory is the psychical equivalent and even the mechanism of resurrection or reincarnation, then it is not forgetting that the *Bhagavad Gita* advocates with the view to exiting the worldly circuits of *saṃsāra*, but the memory of being itself, rather than of this or that kind of being, in the instant preceding death.[28] While *recollection* fleshes out the reversibility of time and the rootedness of the past, *re-presentation* obeys the dynamics of the mind's iterative-modular complexification (more on this later), and anticipatory *projection* into the future follows the lead of opportunistic growth that, in contingent sets of circumstances, calls upon some of the meristems, root tips, and tendrils to leave their state of dormancy.

Reversibility is the overarching theme of the three modalities of time. Durand associates challenges to "ascendant verticality" with "cyclical reciprocity" and, on the same page of his text, with messianic motifs, whereby, for

---

26   Eliade elucidates the intersection of the psychical and the cosmic in the merging of the *chakras* and the *mandala*: "Suffice it to say that the reactivation of the *chakras*—those 'wheels' (or circles) which are regarded as so many points of intersection of the cosmic life and the mental life—is homologous with the initiatory penetration into a *mandala*" (Eliade, *Images and Symbols*, p. 54).

27   In this respect, St. Hildegard notes that "the soul's powers are like the form of a tree [*quasi arboris forma*]" (*Scivias* I.4.26; CCCM 43, p. 84).

28   "Whatever state of being he remembers [*smaran bhāvam*] when he gives up the body at the end, he goes respectively to that state of being, Arjuna, transformed into that state of being" (BG VIII.6). For more on this theme, consult Michael Marder, *The Phoenix Complex: A Philosophy of Nature* (Cambridge, MA: The MIT Press, 2023).

instance, the wood of the cross—as a permutation of the cosmic tree and of the Edenic tree of life—grants salvation at the threshold of death.[29] The past can be rendered future, just as the future becomes the past, not in the sense of a mere succession and endless supplanting of one moment with another, when today's tomorrow becomes the yesterday of the day after tomorrow, but in the precise sense of reversibility: the futurity of the past, which may never be realized or is realized with obvious differences over and over again, and the immemorial pastness of the yet unavailable future. Without being aware of it, though, Durand operates with two types of reversibility, namely the smooth continuation of cyclical rotations and the cataclysmic rupture inherent in a messianic event. How to reconcile them?

The upward vertical thrust of arboreal growth is a tangent of circular or elliptical movement, which, *at the same time*, follows the opposite downward trajectory, as the roots dig further into and through the soil. The "ascendant verticality" underpinning the modern idea of progress as the exclusive vector of historical time with its promise of a reliable and infinite improvement of the future in comparison to the forever-lost past, is, therefore, doubly flawed: (1) still on the vertical axis, it misses the descending portion of plant growth (incomplete verticality), and (2) it overlooks the circumference, of which both of these movements are tangents (incomplete figuration). Apparent ruptures are revealed as moments of a more encompassing, if less than evident, continuity. The event of overturning the "usual" order of things is folded into the workings of this latent order.

In a formulaic fashion, we might say that the reversibility of the cosmic tree and of its time is an offshoot of their being-middle. The reconciliation of opposites (not least, of rupture and continuity) is unnecessary, because the middle in and of itself (which is to say: as other to itself) is the crossing of countervailing forces that swirl there before their polarization at the extremes. Hence, the *kiśkana* tree of ancient Mesopotamia was sometimes rooted in the netherworld and sometimes in the sky, because its ultimate rooting was in the omphalos, the midriff of the world, which is the root of both these roots.

The ramification of the cosmic tree, accounting for the variety and diversity of existents and modes of existence, similarly complicates arboreal verticality.

---

29   Durand cites from the "veneration of the cross" included in the Roman Catholic Good Friday liturgy: "*Ipse lignum tune notavit, Damna ligni ut solveret.*" Other Christian authors have commented on this connection, from Origen and St. Augustine to St. Hildegard of Bingen. "The Cross, made of the wood of the tree of good and evil, appears in the place of this Cosmic Tree" (Eliade, *Images and Symbols*, p. 161).

Branches spread out, lateralizing and rendering horizontal the vertical thrust of the trunk. When the morphology of the tree is inverted, as in *Zohar*, they form the living cupola sheltering terrestrial life, which is one of the senses of the *sefirah šekīnah*, "a branch of those branches planted by the blessed Holy One when He created the world" (1:216b; v. 3, p. 303). The roots, too, are ramified as much as the branches above ground level, leaving only the trunk as the vertical line of mediation between upper and lower ramifications. What does this mean when considering the time dynamics of the cosmic tree?

Ramification in growth is technically called modular development, relying on the reiteration of already existing structures (leaves, twigs, branches, etc.) that complexify plant architectures.[30] These living building blocks are the modules that afford a plant multiple points of access to the outside world by analogy with parallel antennae, receiving and emitting bio-signals in an apparently redundant, replicated pattern. In temporal terms, plant growth illuminates the modularity of the past and the future—multiple parallel pasts and futures that coexist with one another at the level of roots and branches respectively, as well as *within* each of these organs of vegetal morphology. (In some contemporary philosophical discourses, inspired by Nuel Belnap's temporal logic, the term "modal indeterminism" is used in the context of Branching Space-Time, or BST, theory.[31]) The present, as the trunk or the squirrel Ratatösk, who scurries along it in Norse mythology, is a communication channel between the future and the past, the many futures and the many pasts that, through the plant's movement of growth, are spatially expressed, intermingled, parallel to one another and semiautonomous from the growing whole, which *as such*, in the purity of its identity separate from the dispersed plurality of times, does not exist.[32]

Multiple pasts and futures are the temporalities of multiple worlds, whether of the phenomenological worlds (the *Umwelten*) of each existent gathered on the cosmic tree or of the multiverse, as Erwin Schrödinger formulated it in the 1950s.[33] The *aśvattha* tree described in Katha Upaniṣad is in such a way that "all

---

30   Refer to Francis Hallé, *In Praise of Plants* (Portland & London: Timber Press, 2002), p. 108.

31   Refer to Nuel Belnap, Thomas Müller, and Tomasz Placek, *Branching Space-Times: Theory and Applications* (Oxford: Oxford University Press, 2022).

32   In spatial terms, the communication is between the sky and the earth: "The installation and consecration of the sacrificial stake constitute a rite of the Center. Assimilated to the Cosmic Tree, the stake becomes in its turn the axis connecting the three cosmic regions. Communication between Heaven and Earth becomes possible by means of this pillar" (Eliade, *Images and Symbols*, p. 45).

33   "Nearly every result (the quantum theorist) pronounces is about the probability of this *or* that *or* that [...] happening—with usually a great many alternatives. The idea that they

the worlds rest on it" (6.1).[34] Lateralization of arboreal growth; the upper and
the lower ramification of its organs, times, and worlds; the parallel existence of
logically incompatible elements—all these combine to put in doubt Durand's
assertion that "although the tree, like ophidian or zodiacal circles is a measure of time, its verticality makes it a vectorized measure of time, favoring the
ascendant phase of the cycle" and the label he affixes to the presumed privileging of tree verticality as "a one-way vision of time and history."[35]

The ramification of tree organs, between which the trunk extends, disperses
both the beginning and the end among numerous sensitive root tips and meristems devoid of any fundamental stability. The firm trunk, reminiscent of a
phallic column or fire in a merging of the organic and inorganic representations
of a cosmic tree,[36] is equally dynamic in its capacity of a mediator between
polarized extremes and of the middle, preceding all figures of beginnings
and ends in the absence of a unified origin. There is no good justification for
treating it as the central and unsurpassable path of communication, since, by
means of biochemical exudates, leaves and roots can communicate with other
leaves and roots without the assistance of the trunk. What presents itself visu-
ally as a continuous whole is a discontinuous, loosely articulated assemblage,
where two types of reversibility, the cyclical and the ruptured, are intimately

---

be not alternatives but all really happen simultaneously seems lunatic to him, just impossible." Qtd. in Michel Bitbol, *Schrödinger's Philosophy of Quantum Mechanics* (Dodrecht:
Kluwer, 1996), p. 127.

34   *The Early Upaniṣads: Annotated Text and Translation*, translated and edited by Patrick
Olivelle (Oxford & New York: Oxford University Press, 1998), p. 399. Refer also to Eliade,
Patterns in Comparative Religion, p. 273.

35   Durand, *The Anthropological Structures of the Imaginary*, pp. 332–333. Durand expresses
here a uniquely French twentieth-century reductionist view of arboreality as vertical and
ascendant. Aside from Deleuze and Guattari's critique of hierarchical tree logic, which
they oppose to rhizomatic assemblages, Paul Claudel suggests that "in nature, the tree
alone is vertical, along with man" [Paul Claudel, *La connaissance de l'Est* (Paris: Gallimard,
2000), p. 148].

36   Durand, *The Anthropological Structures of the Imaginary*, p. 328ff. At the same time, the
matrix of sexual difference associated with the cosmic tree is more complicated than its
classification as an example of phallic/masculine sexuality would suggest. Mircea Eliade
documents the close ties between the great goddess and the tree: "All over Africa and
in India sap-filled trees symbolize divine motherhood, and are therefore venerated by
women, as well as sought out by the spirits of the dead who want to return to life. The god-
dess-tree motif, whether or not it is completed by the presence of heraldic animals, was
preserved in Indian iconography, whence, though not without gaining a certain admix-
ture of water-cosmogony ideas, it passed into popular art, where we still find it to-day"
(*Patterns in Comparative Religion*, p. 281). The focus on feminine symbolism of the tree
dilutes the phallocentric obsession with the "ascendant phase" of growth, which often
figures in Durand's work.

connected. Ramified, the cosmic tree starts comes to resemble a river with its tributaries in yet another *complexio oppositorum*, the coincidence of opposites at the heart of mystical, magical, alchemical, and vegetal thinking. The riverine and fiery cosmic tree reconciles the seemingly antagonistic elements of water and fire, not to mention a single universe-wide organism and an ecosystem.[37]

• • •

Although plants celebrate in the very fabric of their existence the reconciliation of water and fire, it is the latter element that is exceptionally relevant to the figuration of the cosmic tree and to its ramified temporality of parallel pasts and futures. In addition to the fragments of Heraclitus that raise fire to the level of universality, precisely as a mediator of all exchanges (consult Fragment 90: "All things are an equal exchange for fire and fire for all things [*puros te antamoibē ta panta kai pur apantōn*], as goods are for gold and gold for goods"[38]), ancient Greek cosmos *is* fire, a shining ornament and an order, a brilliant surface appearance and a latent arrangement of things. After all, invoking a cosmic tree in diverse traditions, we (still or already) speak Greek, perhaps without realizing it, and return to the cosmos of the Greeks rather than the much more abstract Latin universe (*universus, universitas*).

Heraclitus draws attention to the shimmering of cosmic fire, rhythmic and measured, as in Fragment 30: "fire everlasting, kindling in measures and going out in measures [*pur aeizōon, aptomenon metra kai aposbennumenon metra*]."[39]

---

37   In the Chinese late Chou and Han literature, "cosmic trees are connected with rivers flowing from the *K'un lun* [the mountain range that represents the *axis mundi* in Chinese mythology]." [Anneliese Bulling, *The Meaning of China's Most Ancient Art* (Leiden: Brill, 1952), p. 100]. Such a connection is even stronger in the Buryat shamanism in Siberia, reaching its climax in the identity of the cosmic tree and river: "The world-pole or world-tree symbol alternates in shamanistic ideology with the world-river symbol, which in some cultures is identical with the river of death" (Ake Hultkrantz, "Ecological and Phenomenological Aspects of Shamanism," in *Shamanism: Critical Concepts in Sociology*, Vol. 3, edited by Andrei Znamenski (New York & London: Routledge, 2003), p. 150). Often, *Zohar* will present Torah, in its cosmic dimension, as the tree of life, as the entire sefirotic tree, or as the trunk of this tree, the *sefirah tif'eret*. In the space of a single page (2:60b), it is asserted, for example, "*Water* is nothing but Torah" and "*Tree* is nothing but Torah, as is written: 'She is a tree of life for those who grasp her'" (v. 4, pp. 320–1).

38   Heraclitus, "Fragments." In G.S. Kirk & J.E. Raven, *The Presocratic Philosophers*, p. 199.

39   Kirk & Raven, *The Presocratic Philosophers*, p. 199. See also Plato's *Timaeus* (30b): "one must say that this cosmos is a living being, ensouled and intelligent [*dei legein tonde ton kosmon zōion empsukhon ennoun*]." In another context, Eliade notes that "the rhythms of cosmic life pursue their normal course so long as the circulation of these opposite and complementary principles is proceeding without hindrance" (Eliade, *Images and Symbols*, p. 128).

The measures in question are those not so much of time as of *temporalization*, neither "within" nor "outside" the order of time. They are the intervals of the rhythmic diminution and augmentation experienced by cosmic "fire everlasting [*pur aeizōon*]," of the fiery living being, *zōon*, that is the cosmos, its order and ornamentation referring to the ornamentation and order of life.

The everlasting nature of cosmic fire makes it a special kind of living being, however: it requires no nourishment and no reproduction, the two activities, to which all plants and animals resort in order to renew themselves either in themselves or in the other who issues from their bodies. Physiologically, time is a function of these two activities, of metabolism and metamorphosis or homomorphism. The fire here below, too, behaves like a living being nourishing itself on oxygen and the materials it burns in, reproducing itself by sending sparks and engulfing areas previously unaffected by it, and gradually dying out in cinders and ashes. But cosmic fire, the cosmos *qua* fire, lacks neither nourishment nor reproduction, the processes reserved for finite beings.[40] It is, like the eternal *aśvattha* tree or the ramified "River of Already [*Kvar*]," which is the aquatic shape of the cosmic tree in *Zohar* (1:6b; v. 1, p. 39), immeasurable according to an index of temporality, because it continuously generates and contains the measures of time in itself.

With regard to actual vegetation, fire does more than ravage forests and fields; it ramifies and reverses time, its modular iterations engendering parallel and intertwined pasts and futures of plants and animals, the earth and the atmosphere. The fire of the sun stimulates growth, driving photosynthesis in plants, who convert solar energy into chemical energy, nourishing themselves on it. The physical augmentation of their bodies is due, in large part, to the transformations of the fire of the sun they have received.[41] When the long-decayed (liquified, gasified or congealed) vegetal matter is extracted from the

---

40   Eliade's equation of "inexhaustible life" and immortality with respect to the cosmic tree might be too precipitous: the difference between them has to do with the infinity of time as opposed to a timeless reality. "We may note at once that the tree represents—whether ritually and concretely, or in mythology and cosmology, or simply symbolically—the living cosmos, endlessly renewing itself. Since inexhaustible life is the equivalent of immortality, the tree-cosmos may therefore become, at a different level, the tree of 'life undying'" (Eliade, *Patterns in Comparative Religion*, p. 267).

41   I have explored this line of thought in my *Green Mass* (2021). For example, "the woods may certainly burn, as they do more and more frequently and devastatingly in the age of global warming, when a spark is enough to ignite them in extremely dry conditions. But, in themselves, they are already fire—the heat and the light of the sun captured, transformed, and perhaps decelerated. [...] What we readily identify as raging fire is quick. Vegetation is slow fire in a winding series of negotiations with the quick solar blaze. Our world is a footnote to these negotiations" (p. 97).

bowels of the earth and set alight again in energy-generating combustion, it is enlivened, for one brief moment, by fire. The cumulative effects of this ghostly reanimation that releases large quantities of CO_2 into the atmosphere reverse the activities of living plants, who fill the air with oxygen, alongside CO_2.[42]

The fires that plants receive, that they dynamically are, and that they are engulfed by millions of years after their life on this planet had come to an end follow rhythms and tempos that may be synchronous, asynchronous, or inverted. Solar fire belongs to the time of planetary rotations and seasonal changes, which I have discussed under the heading of vegetal hetero-temporality in *Plant-Thinking*.[43] Mutually exclusive, the times of vegetative growth and sexual reproduction are the embodied interpretations of the blaze that, having energized plants, is slowed down and transformed, even as plants receive their cues for the optimal timeslots for these activities, in part, from the decreasing or increasing lengths of daylight. The time of decay grazes the upper portion of deep geological time and, in shorter spans, the enrichment of topsoil, rendered appropriate for future growth. The time of "reanimation" calls, again in the language of fire, upon vegetal fossils to serve the needs of industrial production and consumption, to which it is tightly bound. The epoch of global heating is the afterlife of the afterlife of fire, received by plants and the earth, which they become, and released into the atmosphere in the form of particulate matter that lingers on as the residue of combustion.

What are the futures of the solar blaze? They are ramified and simultaneous, despite their occasional incompatibility: the growing plants and the reproducing plants, the burning forests and the combusted vegetal matter that came from the deep past. Their differentiation and ramification are not, for all that, mutually indifferent: incinerated forests may, in the short term, stimulate agricultural production; mass burning of fossil fuels stymies vitality outside the vegetal kingdom. What are the pasts of solar fire? By and large, they intersect with the futures, but also, conspicuously spatialized, come to visibility in the increasing volumes and dimensions of living trees that archive the histories of their nutrients (both those procured by their roots and those obtained from solar energy) in and as their bodies, measuring the annual cycle with another sort of ring: the tree ring. The turning of the cycle remolds the past into the future and the future into the past, the roots into the shoots and the shoots into the roots.

• • •

---

42   D. S. Schimel, "Terrestrial Ecosystems and the Carbon Cycle." *Global Change Biology*, 1(1), 1995, pp. 77–91. More on this ghostly reanimation later.

43   See Marder, *Plant-Thinking*, pp. 95–106.

Readers will protest that we have veered far off course with respect to the cosmic tree in our musings on the times, tempos, and rhythms of fire. Nevertheless, we have now seen, as though in a short animation, the temporalizing workings of the cosmic tree, its constitutive relation with fire, and the more or less unacknowledged permutations of the One in the many with respect to both of these figures. The oneness of the cosmic tree is paradoxical: though one of a kind, it is not a sealed off totality, as an animal organism would be, but a *one* that is inherently many, distinct from "forms of a living unity [which] cannot be divided without losing life." For, Jean-Henri Fabre adds, rehashing the thinking of Aristotle in *Parva naturalia*,[44] "a tree can be subdivided into distinct new plants that produce branches; in turn, the branches can continue to grow as long as they contain buds, but the bud itself is not divisible; it is destroyed by being split up. The vegetable individual is thus a bud."[45] Such an individual is a singular plural being, as Jean-Luc Nancy has it,[46] and a singular plural time, this being *as* this time.

The relation of the One and the many, the individual and the collective, in vegetal life holds in store crucial implications for the cosmic tree and the image of time it yields. Cosmic [tree] time is not a totality, which swallows up all that is in the manner of Kronos eating his children. It is, on the contrary, a set of budding, growing, reproducing, and decaying temporalities, belonging to various kinds of existence, the time of an essentially superficial exteriority, not of lethal interiorization. Time has no stomach, but it has roots, and branches, and leaves. There is, in effect, no Time, just as there is no Tree. And that *there is no* ..., understood in the positive, fertile, infinitely giving sense, *is* the One. The cosmic tree is trees, and time is times, every instant (or, more precisely, the energy carried by what will have become an instant)—a bud on its branches. The spacetime continuum is constrained and shaped by the distribution of matter and energy,[47] curving this or that way and branching out into this tree.

Since the cosmos is alive through and through, since it is not static despite occasional assertions that even in its vegetal form it has an everlasting life, it is necessary to reactive the already mentioned Greek verb (*kosmein*) behind the

---

44   "The plant possesses potential root and stock [*echei kai rizan kai kaulon dunamei*] in every part" (467a23–24) and that, therefore, "the vital principle exists potentially [*archē dunamei*] in every part of the plant" (467a29–30).

45   Qtd. in Hallé, *In Praise of Plants*, p. 110.

46   Jean-Luc Nancy, *Being Singular Plural*, translated by Robert Richardson and Anne O'Byrne (Stanford: Stanford University Press, 2000).

47   "The distribution of matter and energy *constrains* the geometry of space-time but does not *determine* it" [Tim Maudin, *Philosophy of Physics: Space and Time* (Princeton & Oxford: Princeton University Press, 2012), p. 139].

noun. In the gerundive, rather than an arrangement and a shining ornament, the living cosmos is the arranging and the arranged, the ornamenting and the ornamented. An arrayal, cosmos is an ordering, which presupposes an ongoing re- and dis-ordering, befitting the variable brilliance, shimmering diminution and augmentation, of its fire. This, perhaps, is the crux of its difference from the utterly static *taxis*, the other Greek word for order. A tree is also a permanent self-rearranging, decaying in some of its parts and flourishing in others, blossoming, leafing, yielding fruit, whose ripeness is already a prelude to rotting. In keeping with some accounts of the world tree, it is equally subject to the dynamics of decay: Yggdrasil "in its side [...] rots, / Nidhögg beneath tears it," while the "great growing plant" that is the cosmos in Plotinus is, in its lower sections, consumed as though by maggots (*Ennead* IV.3.4, 25–35). Cosmic [tree] time is the tempo of cosmic self-reordering and self-disordering, which, neither centralized nor uniform, proceeds asynchronously in its distinct parts.

CHAPTER 4

Diachrony, Sexual Difference, and Other Plant Matters

Plants are among the pioneers of sexuality in the history of life. Before them, the first living beings who invented sex two billion years ago were bacteria. Although their genetic exchanges sometimes fall in the category of parasexuality, bacteria are capable of conjugation, transformation, and transduction, relations that even include "sex without reproduction"—namely, conjugation, or a temporary union of two "conjugants" exchanging genetic material and then separating.[1] So, bacteria engage in sexual play, which is not subordinated to the teleological demands of procreation. The sheer volume of flowers produced by a cherry tree beyond what is strictly needed for reproduction may also be a sign of playful sexual display, as Friedrich Schiller intuited in the nineteenth century.[2]

In many plant species, sexual reproduction coexists with asexual reproduction, which, in this case, is called "facultative."[3] The main difference between the two kinds of reproduction is that sexual reproduction introduces new genetic variations into a population, while asexual reproduction produces clones. An exception to this rule of thumb is that sexual reproduction can have clonal outcomes in plants in the case of self-fertilization; however, the possibilities of self-fertilization are minimized via the mechanisms of self-incompatibility, inhibiting the hydration of pollen received in the process.[4] When plants have sexual reproduction at their disposal, they will seek to maximize genetic diversity and the ever-proliferating versions of otherness.

---

1   Giuseppe Fusco and Alessandro Minelli, *The Biology of Reproduction* (Cambridge: Cambridge University Press, 2019), pp. 37–38, 42.
2   "The tree puts forth innumerable buds which perish without developing, and stretches out for nourishment many more roots, branches, and leaves than are used for the maintenance of itself and its species. What the tree returns from its lavish profusion unused and unenjoyed to the kingdom of the elements, the living creature may squander in joyous movements" Friedrich Schiller, *On the Aesthetic Education of Man*, translated by Reginald Snell (Mineola, NY: Dover, 2004), p. 133.
3   Fusco & Minelli, *The Biology of Reproduction*, p. 14.
4   Megumi Iwano, et al, "Self-Incompatibility in the Brassicaceae." In *Sexual Reproduction in Animals and Plants*, edited by Hitoshi Sawada, Naokazu Inoue and Megumi Iwano (London: Springer, 2014), pp 245–246.

Focusing on vegetal sexuality, we notice that it renders the time of plants diachronous. When plants are in the phase of vegetative growth, they do not develop new reproductive organs, such as the flowers; when plants are in the phase of sexual reproduction, their vegetative growth slows down. Plant scientists explain this tendency by the mechanisms of differential "reproductive allocation." "Observations of a negative effect of current reproduction on current growth" are attributable to the physical costs of reproduction.[5] Since there are "limited amounts of time or energy available for expenditure,"[6] the allocation of resources needs to happen in such a way that they are channeled toward one type of activity and away from another type. The "temporal separation between reproductive and somatic allocations" means that resources cannot be stored for future use, due to various "costs of storage," above all the possibility that energy-rich plant organs where they are hoarded would be consumed by animals.[7]

In reproductive allocation theories, not only energy but also time is conceived as a resource, rather than as the dialectical unity of two opposite phases.[8] Nevertheless, time is a dubious resource, given its diachronous character in sexually reproducing plants. In this context, time entails an alternation, reflected in the nuclear structure, whereby most plants are haplodiplontic: "in this life cycle there are two phases, one haploid, the other diploid, neither of which is transitory."[9] There is here a clear alternation of generations with a distinction in ploidy—or the number of sets of chromosomes—between a haploid gamete and diploid spore-producing sporophyte. Haplodiploidy encapsulates the opposition between growth and sexual reproduction: spores grow, whereas gametes fuse.

The unsettling fact that calendar time is inapplicable (and, indeed, subordinate) to reproductive time is evident in the concept of generation. In light of its definition as *"a set of individuals that come into being through reproduction,"* where *n*th generation is *"the set of individuals generated through* n *reproductive events starting from an individual or a parent pair,"* "two seeds of sequoia produced by the same mother plant 2000 years apart belong to the same generation."[10] Two millennia can thus be condensed into the same generation

5   P. Steffan Karlsson & Marcos Mendez, "The Resource Economy of Plant Reproduction." In *Reproductive Allocation in Plants*, edited by Edward Reekie & Fakhri A. Bazzaz (Amsterdam: Elsevier, 2005), p. 2.

6   M.L. Cody, "A General Theory of Clutsch Size." *Evolution*, 20 (1966), pp. 174–184.

7   Karlsson & Mendez, "The Resource Economy of Plant Reproduction," pp. 22, 27.

8   "When the principle of allocation was formulated, two kinds of resources were in focus, energy and time" (Karlsson & Mendez, "The Resource Economy of Plant Reproduction," p. 6).

9   Fusco & Minelli, *The Biology of Reproduction*, p. 48.

10   Fusco & Minelli, *The Biology of Reproduction*, p. 18.

thanks to the long lifespan of a tree, during which its fecundity is kept in tact. More importantly still, the biological notion of generation encourages a reinterpretation of time on the basis of reproductive sexuality and its ground rules. The time of reproduction is no longer a stretch or a particular period within the general flow of time; rather, time itself stretches and contracts, dilates and dwindles, rhythmically alternates between two or more phases in keeping with the vicissitudes of vegetative and sexual reproductive activities.

· · ·

At this point, I am obliged to retrace my steps with greater care. How do the peculiarities of plant sexuality determine the time of plants, let alone time *as such*? If not even plants that reproduce asexually follow the alternating rhythms of reproduction and growth (since, for them, growth *is* reproduction and vice versa), then why would the innermost dynamic of time be consistent with a relatively late evolutionary invention?

I can think of several overlapping answers to the above questions. First, the contrapuntal forms of time stand for continuity and discontinuity, sameness and otherness, their combination making time what it is. The mutual interruption of the two moments is a sequential movement; their sequence is an interrupted, broken line. Each taken by itself is tantamount to atemporal time, be it the seamless continuity of growth or the relentless punctuations of sexual reproduction. Paradoxically, then, there is no time before the advent of sexuality!

In the case of asexual (or vegetative) reproduction, genetically identical clones proliferate in the absence of any internal time limits, either in symmetric binary fission "where the parent's body is divided equally between the two offspring individuals" or in an asymmetric fashion, "such as budding, where the parent persists as a distinct individual across the reproductive act while a minor portion of its body becomes the offspring."[11] At least potentially, within this framework, the time of the living abuts eternity. Likewise, sexual reproduction detached from the phase of vegetative growth produces pollen or seeds that, in theory, indefinitely preserve the potentiality of germination or growth. Time stops. And, on the contrary, for it to proceed, time must keep to a halting rhythm of a ruptured continuation and a continued rupture, figured or configured in the phases of sexual and asexual reproduction.

Second, much in the same sense that, for the ancients and in cosmologies that thrive outside the West, life is not an exception within the overall

---

11   Fusco & Minelli, *The Biology of Reproduction*, p. 15.

existence of the cosmos, sexuality is not an exception in the order of life. One of the last European representatives of this line of thought, Friedrich Schelling writes that "throughout the whole of Nature absolute sexlessness is nowhere demonstrable, and an *a priori* regulative principle requires that sexual difference be taken as a point of departure everywhere in organic nature. [...] As for sexual difference itself, [...] separation into different sexes happens for different organisms at different stages of formation, and this is itself proof for the assumption that each organism has a level of formation at which that separation is *necessary*. Nature has either unified the opposing sexes in one and the same product [...], or Nature has distributed the opposing sexes into different stocks (individuals)."[12]

Sexual exchanges among bacteria two billion years ago seem to substantiate Schelling's argument. Here, sexual difference is the default condition of organic life and apparent sexlessness is its temporary suppression. Time is the ebb and flow of the revelation and concealment (or latency, as Freud termed it in the context of human life) of sexual difference (rather than of the apparently neutered Being, as in Heidegger's philosophy), with the peak of revelation taking on the appearance of disruption, discontinuity, upheaval in and punctuation of "routine" existence. The overall vegetal movement that is *phusis* is, thus, not only a budding outgrowth of the same, but also, and at the same time that makes room for time or for times, a disruption of this burgeoning outpouring by way of sexuality.

Third, the hesitancies, equivocations, and pendular swings within sexual difference and between sexual difference and its opposite in vegetal life convey the non-teleological, occasion-specific nature of plant ontology and of the time of plants, while indicating that there is no stiff division between alternative modes of reproduction. In "gender diphasy," plants choose their sex, for instance, according to "the supply of resources available for reproduction."[13] "The terms 'sex changing,' 'labile sexuality,' 'sex reversal,' 'sex choice,' 'phase choice,' 'alternative gender,' 'sequential gender,' 'sequential cosexuality,' and 'sequential hermaphroditism' have all been used in reference to diphasy."[14] The plasticity of their sexual expression, and of whether or not they intend

---

12   F.W.J. Schelling, *First Outline of a System of the Philosophy of Nature*, translated by Keith R. Peterson (Albany, NY: SUNY Press, 2004), pp. 36–37.

13   Jon Lovett Doust & Lesley Lovett Doust, "Sociobiology of Plants: An Emerging Synthesis." In *Plant Reproductive Ecology*, edited by Jon Lovett Doust & Lesley Lovett Doust (New York & Oxford: Oxford University Press, 1988), p. 14.

14   Mark A. Schlessman, "Gender Diphasy ('Sex Choice'). In *Plant Reproductive Ecology*, edited by Jon Lovett Doust & Lesley Lovett Doust (New York & Oxford: Oxford University Press, 1988), p. 139.

to reproduce sexually or asexually, culminates in the sexual polymorphism of plants.[15] The bodies, relations, and temporalities of plants are invented and reinvented in light of the mutable conditions of their lifeworld. Evolution is "creative," as Henri Bergson suggested, and so is also, at a more basic level, time itself in its congruence with the plasticity of vegetal life.

The instability of sexual difference in plants is, rather than a defect, a sign of their ontological and temporal openness, their incongruity with the structure of the totality. For Hegel, this constitutes a serious problem. In his *Philosophy of Nature*, sexual difference is "only quite partial" in the vegetal kingdom (*"der Unterschied ist so nur ganz partiell"*)[16] for two reasons. Not only is plant sexuality indeterminate and "the differences are very often changeable while plants are growing," but it is also concentrated in the flower, a detachable and superfluous part of plant, *ein abgeschiedener Teil*. "The different individuals," Hegel writes, "cannot therefore be regarded as of different sexes because they have not been completely imbued with the *principle* of their opposition [*sie nicht in daß* Prinzip *ihrer Eingegensetzung ganz eingetaucht find*]—because this does not completely pervade them [*nicht ganz durchbringt*], is not a universal moment of the entire individual [...]."

Stated otherwise, plants are not sufficiently self-negated; the partial manner in which sexual difference is manifest in vegetal life does not result in the actual existence of two opposite sexes. This difference oscillates between the disjunction and the conjunction of the polarities it interrelates, on the one hand, and their irrelevance to asexual reproduction, on the other. Its refinement and determination will require a transition to animal existence, where the entire flesh is awash in sexuality and arranged in oppositional formations of the masculine against the feminine. What Hegel postulates, then, is the necessary animalization of sexual difference through "the principle of opposition" as a sign of the animal's engagement with, interest in, and non-indifference to itself and its other. And he interprets the precarious situation of the plant as that of an indifferent difference: uncommitted, utterly malleable, plastic, fluid due to its presumed lack of involvement, the incapacity to negate itself and its other on a path to the full flowering of subjectivity. The breathtaking freedom of the plant flips, on Hegel's prompting, into a nearly mechanistic partiality, the technicity of and in nature.[17]

---

15   Doust & Doust, "Sociobiology of Plants," p. 7.
16   Hegel, *Philosophy of Nature*, p. 344. Until the next indication, all subsequent quotations are from this page of the text.
17   To the polymorphous sexuality of plants, to their non-oppositionality, Hegel opposes "the principle of opposition," that is, the dialectical principle *par excellence*. The implications

To return to the question of time (or, rather, of times), diachrony is not predicated on the principle of opposition, and it is doubtful, moreover, that it involves any principle whatsoever. In fact, a diachronic rhythm is, in and of itself, unprincipled, irreducible to the simplicity of the One, not unified in a coherent and overarching beginning. Its anarchy does not even admit the principle of no-principle. Within the time frames and environmental factors of reproduction, there is no reason for sexuality (and its interplay with asexuality) to be organized by any sort of principle, let alone that of oppositionality. Dialectically, too, Hegel is, as we have already seen, mistrustful of principles and principal things, of the all-powerful beginnings and origins. Why is his mistrust inapplicable to the principle of opposition and of self-opposition, which is already two in one and one in two?

• • •

Plant sexual ontology condenses in itself all the promises and paradoxes of plant ontology *proper*, vegetal being as the expression of vegetal time. Their slipping away from the principle of opposition liberates plants from two things at once: the dominion of a principle and the logic of oppositionality. This double move is temporalizing: it is at odds with the fiction of an atemporal static identity and with the equally immobile, deadlocked non-identity of pure opposition.

Growing and reproducing in the absence of a single governing rule (say, the "law" of sexual reproduction oblivious to the ever-changing environmental circumstances), plants live anarchically. Wholly temporal, meaning itself blossoms at the pace of their life or lives, full of surprising twists and turns, of differences that are "very changeable," mutable, alterable: *sehr wandelbar*. Plant world is home to different differences, i.e., differences that preclude sameness both in their form and in their content, whereas Hegel strives to

---

of this move are broad. Being oneself has to be interpreted as being against the other, not thriving in contiguity with alterity in the manner of plants; when all is said and done, it is being an animal, animalizing all difference, including, first and foremost, sexual difference. From Hegel's standpoint, not being against the other, the plant is also not itself. Immersed in the immediacy of an affirmation toward the outside, often indistinguishable from the inside, the plant is not bathed in, soaked, permeated (*eingetaucht, durchbringt*) with sexual difference in accordance with the principle of opposition. Or, at least, not totally (*ganz*) so, for this is a matter of partiality and totality: the totality of difference *or* its detachable, easily differentiated expression in a relatively free-standing part. The plant's immersion in pure immanence separates its sexual organs, namely the flowers, from the rest of its body that disobeys the principle of opposition, in and through which difference is registered, organized, and incorporated into organic being. The Hegelian flower is cut *a priori*, culled from the vegetal extension to which it belongs, as it were, by accident, as a playful and not entirely necessary supplement.

set up a dialectic of difference in content and formal sameness, which is the principle of negation and contradiction. By being *too* different in its vegetal version, sexual difference reverts back, in Hegel's eyes, to indifference and non-differentiation, affecting the "genus-process," *Gattungs-Prozeß*, and the life-process of each plant.

How to approach vegetal being, quilted together as it is from different differences, absent a foothold, or a roothold, in sameness?[18] In the case of many kinds of animals and humans, a community consists of a number of individuals; it names a grouping or an assembly comprised of members who are distinct from the collectivity and who, though participating *in* it, maintain their identity *outside* it. The Hegelian point is that, in order to occupy this position inside-out or outside-in, the individual must be imbued with the principle oppositionality, starting with the oppositional organization of sexual difference. The individual as a whole is determined by the possibility of a total negation by the other, with sexuality and death, *eros* and *thanatos*, fleshing out the totality of existential negation, of finitude internalized and, hence, of time internalized. Reproduction in the other is a response to the limit to reproducibility in oneself set by mortality.

The individuals' participation in a community is a return, a conscious taking-hold of, or, in totalitarian systems, a largely unconscious delivering themselves to, the forces responsible for their individuation, and yet also strangely deindivdualizing. First and foremost, their sexual individuation, seeing that "the entire habit (*habitus*) of the individual must be bound up with its sex [*Der ganze Habitus des Individuums muß mit seinem Geschlecht verbunden sein*]," that is to say, with the oppositionality that defines dialectical sexual ontology and dialectics as such. Plants, for their part, are and think differently, indicating an escape route from dialectics within dialectics and putting into question the suffocating totality of community. "The difference reached by the plant, which is a difference of one vegetative self [*einem vegetativen Selbst*] from another vegetative self, each of which has the urge to identify itself with the other—this determination exists only as an analogue of the sexual relation [*ein Analogon des Geschlechts-Verhältnisse*]. For the sides of the relation are not two individuals."

The vegetal is made not of individuals but of super- or infra-individual differences, because the "self" of a plant is not an individual, either. In the flora, sexual difference is a relation involving something more or something less (indeed,

---

18   I note in passing that radical difference is a quality of vegetal subjectivity, which cannot be observed within the context of biology. Evidently, plant cells and DNA do not display that kind of difference, even if they support it with remarkable phenotypic plasticity and, more pertinently, fluid sex determination.

both more *and* less) than two individuals, which, for Hegel, is no longer or not yet a relation, but its "analogue"—the putting into proportion of differences. This proportional measure of differences is time *embodied* in the vegetal variation on the sexual relation. The analogy of the sexual relation slots plants above and below *logos*, the realm of principles and oppositions summed up in the principle of oppositionality. This analogy is diachronous. Circumventing the mediations of *logos*, the vegetal articulation is unsayable, uncontainable in the medium of the voice and inappropriate to a way of assembling thoughts in the formations of contradiction and non-contradiction. Rather than being inside-out or outside-in a community, the plant is completely outside, which, if we follow Hegel, amounts to being completely within, based on the indifference of radical difference.

Besides the extra-individual nature of vegetal existence, which contributes to the misalignment of communal boundaries between this existence and that of animals and humans, the "analogy of the sexual relation" explains the essential superficiality of plant life. Sexualization grants the dialectical subject its form, as well as its specific character. At its crest, only "when the inner, generative forces have reached complete penetration and saturation [*die ganze Durchbringung und Sättigung*], does the individual possess the sexual impulse, and only then is it awakened." The subjective interiority of the animal and the human is a product of the withholding of the sexual impulse within a totality forged by generative forces in a state of "complete penetration and saturation." The individual is permeated by sexual difference, to the point of repletion and satiation, triggering the sexual impulse. Its subjectivity is nothing other than a force (here, the drive, "generative forces") kept at bay, invariably delayed in its expression and inexhaustible in its occasional exteriorizations. Any relation that may emerge from the tensions and outbursts of that accumulated force will happen as a meeting of two or more interiorities, of dark recesses and reserves where each subject will hide, despite and in the course of its exposure to the other.

Conversely, the vegetal relation (or its analogue) will be superficial, receiving a kiss and a caress of sunrays or of water, of a gust of wind or butterfly wings spreading pollen. In its exteriority, it is not an explosion of the normally withheld impulse, but a diachronic alternation that is neither predetermined nor constrained by the dynamics of force and that may or may not happen depending on the environmental conditions at hand. When it does take place, the "analogue of the sexual relation" is a brushing of two or more surfaces that do not occlude a hidden reserve but, instead, open unto the other unreservedly. There might be friction but no opposition there where—in place of the drive, pulsion of force, "an impulse"—one finds "the development of its [the plant's] organs [*daß Bildende seiner Organe*]," the formation and opening of flowers. Flowering toward the other is in stark contrast to penetrating and being penetrated by the other. It delineates a time without interiority, the time flourishing thanks to a kiss and a caress that are elemental, cross-kingdoms and cross-species, or, within the same species, happen between genetically diverse or identical parties to a relation.

· · ·

Hegel is bad at finding his bearings in exteriority, which, to him, is suggestive of space, instead of time. Devoid of opposition, vegetal difference becomes indistinguishable from indifference, otherness from sameness, unconditional openness to the other from absolute closure. So much so that Hegel denies the sexual difference of plants: "The plant therefore is asexual [*Geschlechtlos*], even the *Dioecia*, because the sexual parts form a closed, separate circle [*eine abgeschlossenen, besonderen Kreis*] apart from their individuality."[19]

Beyond dialectical being, concretized across its self-negations and self-determinations that commence with its abstract opposition to nothing, there is but non-being; outside the confines of dialectical thought—only non-thought. To be sure, Hegel could not have known about phytoestrogens and complex hormonal networks traversing the bodies of plants and carrying these and other hormones well beyond the flowers, thus rendered not so detachable from the rest of the plant. But this is not a good excuse. Undergirding his use of botanical data at the cutting edge of nineteenth-century science is a double methodological thrust I have already pointed out: (1) to cull the flower from the rest of the vegetal body, whose asexual and deathless non-individuated limits it transgresses and (2) by culling the flower, to cut the plant from relationality, from a possible model of community, and from time.

Why then read *Philosophy of Nature*, Part II of the *Encyclopaedia of the Philosophical Sciences* in "our" twenty-first century, given that the author of this treatize seems to preclude the more just, inclusive, ecologically and socially sensitive ways of articulating the common? Because dialectical reason works behind Hegel's back: in addition to co-opting and neutralizing, it promotes the vectors of liberation, among them the vegetal and the communal. And it elucidates the relationality of time.

Take, for instance, the early formulation of sexual difference in plants in Paragraph 348: "But the plant does not attain to a relationship between individuals as such [*als solcher*] but only to a difference, whose sides are not at the same time in themselves whole individuals [...]; therefore, the difference,

---

19   Hegel, *Philosophy of Nature*, p. 345.

too, does not go beyond a beginning [*einem Beginn*] and an adumbration of the genus-process."[20] A relationship between individual terms recedes to the background in the measure that the terms are individuated and foregrounded, obstructing with their definite outlines the very relation they participate in; in other words, they leave no room for relationality or difference "in themselves," which is to say "in the other." Plants, however, attain to a difference underlying any relation, a silent word underwriting all speech, the time of a divergence, time *qua* divergence.

I wonder, at the same time, what would have happened, were Hegel's *Philosophy of Nature* to transition not only from vegetality to animality, but also from animality ("the animal organism," with which it culminates) to humanity, and were it to do so precisely as a philosophy of nature, rather than a phenomenology of spirit. How would the manifold differences in sexual difference have appeared? In which light would they have been cast? Which mode of *temporalization by sexual difference* would prevail?

One conjecture is that, as soon as it is humanized, sexual difference will be wrapped in tragedy. Already an animal experiences sexuality as the embodied principle of opposition, permeating the entire organism, and, therefore, as "the negative power [*die negative Macht*] over the individual, realized through the sacrifice of this individual which it replaces by another."[21] The time it incarnates is the time of mortality, of the impending death, mitigated by the birth of the offspring. The negative power, which produces the individual by turning the self against itself and against its other, consumes its product in the species, to which the organism is subordinated. A *we* gains an upper hand over the *I*, if only by adding another *I* meant to replace the first. Resolving the opposition of sexual difference in progeny is not a happy synthesis but, on the contrary, intergenerational sacrifice, continuing to fuel dialectical frictions between the singular and the universal.

As for the human, sexual difference reaches over into the legal and political spheres (hence, *Philosophy of Right*), where the opposition between the masculine and the feminine comes to a head. In *Phenomenology of Spirit*, Creon and Antigone enact the tragic dimension that exacerbates the power of negativity palpable in animal sexuality. Sublimated, the principle of oppositionality that saturates a sexed body spills over into distinct conceptions, practices, and temporalities of communal being with irreconcilable demands laid on the subject: the family and a living tradition *versus* the state and a deadening law.[22]

---

20 Hegel, *Philosophy of Nature*, p. 343.

21 Hegel, *Philosophy of Nature*, p. 346.

22 In *Philosophy of Right*, the families gathered in civil society perform a mediating function between these extremes and, in their multiplicity as well as the middling position between the family and the state, play a vegetal role in the process.

Because Hegel considers the generic character of sexual difference in plants to be "formal," and so immune to internal negation and to permeation by the spirit of opposition, he concedes that the element of sacrifice is absent from vegetal sexuality. Instead of negative power, the plant incarnates "this positive side," *diese positive Seite*, of the genus-process, which is one and the same as its "relationship to the outer world."[23] Its individuality is a collectivity, and its collectivity—an individuality oriented toward exteriority. The self-production of a vegetal living being is its reproduction in the other, and its replacement by another is an affirmation of the heteronomous self. This is not a synthesis nor an immediate coincidence of opposites that do not have a place in vegetal life. Rather, the mutual predication of reproduction in the self and in the other is wholly temporal; more than that, it is diachrony itself.

The positive side of the vegetal genus process that knows no sacrifice is, in the end, "the only necessary side of the negation [*allein nötige Seite der Negation*]"[24] oblivious to dialectical mediations. *Too* different, it lapses into sameness. Here, not only does the same masquerade as the other, but also negation poses as absolute positivity. So, whereas the animal or animalized iterations of sexual difference are tragic, the vegetal varieties are comic, full of sudden reversals, mishmashes, and confusions—again, a little like time itself. (In *Phenomenology of Spirit*, Hegel asserts that plants were the living enablers of the "mingling" or "blending," *Vermischung*, of natural forms and forms of thought—hence, what I refer to as plant-thinking." For Hegel, though, all such mingling is "unthinking").[25] The comic element of vegetal sexuality resides in these confusions and immediate identifications of extremes as much as in "playful superfluity"[26] and contingency, given that the plant can reproduce itself without resorting to sexual difference. The sexual interplay of bacteria that took place two billion years ago resurfaces in vegetal sexuality, *as* vegetal sexuality.

Given how intimately sexual difference is tied to ontology and temporal unfolding, the surface-oriented and the subjectively deep, the comic and the tragic, the playful and the sacrificial overtones of sexuality will variously mold both being and time. The tragic and relentless march to one's end, albeit not without leaving progeny behind in order to survive in one way or another the end of oneself, needs to be counterbalanced with the comic and diachronic back-and-forth, incompatible with the teleology of personal and collective histories. The senses of human being and time come into sharper relief in this context, mindful of the animal and the vegetal, the tragic and the comic sense of existence.

---

23   Hegel, *Philosophy of Nature*, p. 346.
24   Hegel, *Philosophy of Nature*, p. 347.
25   Hegel, *Hegel's Phenomenology of Spirit*, pp. 427, 449.
26   Hegel, *Philosophy of Nature*, p. 345.

Deepening the tragic standoff of animal sexuality, humankind has not yet become human; if anything—and much like family, society, law, politics and other ingredients of the Hegelian right (*Recht*)—it has been hyper-animalized. Becoming human does not require a vehement rejection of a rich non-human heritage, but, on the contrary, enjoins us to draw on more of this heritage, especially on the repressed vegetal dimension of sexual difference. The challenge is to embrace the plant and the animal, surface and depth, play and work, non-oppositionality and oppositionality in a condition that is essentially tragicomic. To juggle what Nietzsche derided as "bearish seriousness" and flowery levity. Diachrony is the irreducibility of either dimension, of either temporality that makes time what it is.

•••

The fundamental tension between totality and infinity in Emmanuel Levinas's thought is a matter of time. To be precise, it is a tension between the entirely continuous time of retention and protention, as charted in Husserl's model of internal time consciousness, on the one hand, and of the discontinuous temporality of the unrepresentable, the immemorial, that which cannot be anticipated. We have come across the vegetal connotations of phenomenological time consciousness, sprouting from the middle (of the present and ever so partial presence) without a clear origin or principle. Nevertheless, this figure, privileging vegetative growth, does not account for the fissures and gaps that open thanks to sexual reproduction and its effects. My argument is that the diachrony of time in Levinas's work ought to be understood as the mutually disrupting vegetal temporalities of growth and sexual reproduction, with their divergent relations to alterity.

Plants not only exist in two words simultaneously, thriving above and below ground, but also live in two times, which cannot be synchronized with one another. Vegetal diachrony, far from a failure of synchronization, means that time cannot be synchronized with itself. Occasionally, Levinas describes the diachrony "restored to time" as coming in touch with "nocturnal time," which cannot be processed by the apparatus of internal time consciousness: "Forgetting restores diachrony to time. A diachrony without protention or retention. To wait for nothing and to forget everything, the opposite of subjectivity, 'absence of all center'."[27] Whereas time as such is an "astonishing divergence of

---

27   Emmanuel Levinas, "The Servant and Her Master." In *The Levinas Reader*, edited by Sean Hand (Oxford & Cambridge: Blackwell, 1989), p. 155.

the identical from itself,"[28] this divergence varies: it may be relative or absolute. In the continuous flows of inner time consciousness that retain a past present in memory and project a future present in anticipation, it is relative; in absolute forgetting and an awaiting of nothing, it is absolute. Diachrony breaks out in this second, absolute divergence of the identical from itself, which is allied to the absolute other: "obedience to the absolute other" is "the diachrony of the future itself."[29] But it also introduces a wedge between the first, relative, divergence and the second, absolute, divergence; growth and sexual reproduction; the time of transferred, transited presence and the time of the immemorial past and the uncertain future.

Overviewed from the perspective of continuous growth, the disruptions of sexual reproduction are signs of absence; from the vantage of internal time consciousness, the non-representable past and future are pure losses. "Does the diachrony of time signify only deficiency of presence and nostalgia?" Levinas asks.[30] If so, then it is "as if time, in its diachrony came down to a failed eternity."[31] The growth that comes to the fore with the focus on the processes of retention and protention blocks from sight the positivity of what does not fit within its parameters. But sexual reproduction that is foregrounded at the expense of growth also erases the extensions of time in retention and protention, the stretch or the stretching of consciousness and its finite luminosity. Hence, Levinas admires "the *diachrony* of the future in that irreversible subjection that does not become inverted into knowledge and that, as if inspired, signifies *beyond* that which, in obedience, can be represented and presented."[32] Instead of relations of reversibility and irreversibility (where, whether symmetrically or asymmetrically, each reduces the two, the dyad of diachrony, to one), it would have been more appropriate to invoke the oscillations between times, between modalities of the future as protention and the unknown to-come, as Derrida indeed does in Levinas's footsteps.

Levinas struggles to express these diachronic oscillations in *Totality and Infinity*, notably in the section of the book dedicated to the issue of "fecundity." "My child is a stranger [*mon enfant est un étranger*]," he writes with reference to *Isaiah* 49, "but a stranger who is not only mine, for he *is* me. He is me a stranger to myself. [...] No anticipation represents him [*Aucune anticipation ne le*

28   Emmanuel Levinas, *Otherwise Than Being or Beyond Essence*, translated by Alphonso Lingis (Dodrecht: Kluwer, 1991), p. 28.
29   Emmanuel Levinas, *Alterity and Transcendence*, translated by Michael B. Smith (London: The Athlone Press, 1999), p. 34.
30   Levinas, *Alterity and Transcendence*, p. 16.
31   Levinas, *Alterity and Transcendence*, p. 13.
32   Levinas, *Alterity and Transcendence*, p. 36.

représente] nor, as is said today, projects him. [...] Both my own and non-mine, a possibility of myself but also a possibility of the other, of the Beloved, my future does not enter into the logical essence of the possible. The relation with such a future [*avenir*], irreducible to the power over possibles, we shall call fecundity."[33]

Still formulated with an eye to the future, diachrony takes the shape of undulations between appropriation and the non-appropriable, concentrated in the offspring (and, above all, the time of the offspring) who is both mine and non-mine. Sexual difference drives the impossibility of a straightforward appropriation, not only because the child is individually distinct from the progenitor, but also because the child is a crossing of possibilities of both parents, in addition to the unique possibilities that are her or his own. Individual distinctness and the ruptured continuation or the continued rupture unfolding between "me" and the stranger that I am to myself in and as my child—in a word, diachrony as a precondition for difference—hinge upon the non-appropriable possibility of the other other, who is "the Beloved." Sexual difference is, therefore, a breaking point in the otherwise sealed logic of the totality (of growth, of conscious retentions and protentions, etc.) unable to accommodate the oscillations of fecundity. To reiterate, with Levinas: such an "inability to accommodate" is, more than a negative and prohibitive limit, the very movement of temporalization, that is, of diachronization.

In vegetal life, where the diachrony of reproduction in oneself or in the other is an open-ended experimentation responsive among other things to changing environmental conditions, the difference between mine and non-mine is uncertain *ab initio*. Plants do not start from the possessive or appropriative blueprint of subjectivity, not least because they do not operate with a rigid distinction between the inside and the outside, the same and the other.[34] It is in this vein that we may interpret the somewhat dry scientific observation regarding the futility (if not the dangers) of accumulating and storing resources for future use in the event of sexual reproduction. Corresponding to a non-possessive vegetal subjectivity is a mode of knowing without representations, which problematizes the lines of demarcation Levinas draws between the unknowable future and anticipations reliant on the work of protention. Does this not mean that, irreducible to a "simple" extension of the same material being or conscious process, growth, too, is diachronic? Assuming this to be the case, diachrony would infiltrate, beyond the relation between reproduction in oneself and in the other, into each of these two moments themselves.

---

33   Emmanuel Levinas, *Totality and Infinity: An Essay on Exteriority*, translated by Alphonso
       Lingis (The Hague: Martinus Nijhoff Publishers, 1979), p. 267.

34   On the blurring of these distinctions in plant life, see my *Plant-Thinking*.

Vegetal diachrony, expressed on the nuclear plane in haplodiploidy, is the diachrony of time as such—the "as such" not taken as an empty form or an abstract and transcendental condition of possibility for experience, but as an always already figured, configured, configuring and self-reconfiguring assemblage. To grasp diachrony in abstract terms would be to repeat *mutatis mutandis* the Kantian gesture, according to which space is all at once, while time is successive or sequential. Broadly conceiving the diachrony of time in terms of an escape from the totality of space, Levinas runs the risk of letting his insights dissipate in the rarefied atmosphere of post-Kantian thought.[35] That is why the diachrony of time requires a concretization and a materialization in fecundity and the figure of the child. Nonetheless, before a human child, the offspring, issue, or progeny is animal and vegetal, fungal and bacterial, where a crucial difference—the difference that makes all the difference—is not engrained in systems of classification and taxonomies accentuating divergences among and within kingdoms, classes, and species, but sexual difference (as well as the unstable difference between this difference and its apparent absence).

Levinas's formulations in *Totality and Infinity* gain precision when he notes that fecundity "articulates the time of the absolutely other" and that "transcendence is time and goes unto the other [*La transcendence est temps et va vers Autrui*]."[36] The articulations of time in and by fecundity are, by the same token, its dis-articulations, and this odd logic holds for sexual reproduction as much as for vegetative growth that composes, decomposes, and recomposes itself in loose assemblages, ever ready to fall apart, to undergo disarticulation. It is, in other words, never an ongoing accumulation, never a sheer quantitive increase within a homogeneous totality, nor a unidirectional augmentation of the same. (We might say that a plant is not all leaf, as Goethe had it, but all joint, all meristem.) The retentive and protentive thrust of consciousness, which reiterates in its own way the movement of vegetative growth, is, like this very growth, diachronic through and through.[37]

Ultimately, the ruptured continuity of fecundity is, for Levinas, a way of figuring the infinity of time beyond the Hegelian opposition between the bad infinity of a straight line and the good infinity of a circle. "Fecundity," Levinas

---

35 For instance: "This impossibility of totalization is not purely negative. It traces out a new relation, a diachronic time that no historiography transforms into a totality, thematized simultaneity [...]" (Levinas, *Alterity and Transcendence*, p. 51).

36 Levinas, *Totality and Infinity*, p. 269.

37 And this is true not only in the diluted sense, in which the diachrony of consciousness is "immediately interpreted on the basis of a re-tained or pro-tained, remembered or anticipated presence, as a synchronization of duration in representation" (Levinas, *Alterity and Transcendence*, p. 124).

concludes, "continues history without producing old age [*continue l'histoire sans produire de vieillesse*]. Infinite time does not bring an eternal life to an aging subject; it is *better* across the discontinuity of generations, punctuated by the inexhaustible youths of the child [*les jeunesses inépuisables d'enfant*]."[38] The discontinuity of generations, indebted to sexual reproduction, is contrasted to the presumably vegetative "tedium of [...] repetition [*l'ennui de ce ressassement*]," which ceases in fecundity.[39]

To deal with this tedium more scrupulously, though, diachrony needs to liberate itself from the logic of reproduction—in oneself or in the other, who one both is and is not—and to return to the "inexhaustible youths of the child" as play, the parasexual play of bacteria two billion years ago, the material play of the blossoming tree in Schiller, the "playful superfluity" of vegetal sexuality in Hegel, and so forth. Levinas, for his part, cannot identify anything but the "logical and ontological play of the same and the other," which he finds ethically deplorable. Neither necessarily better nor worse, "across the discontinuity of generations," play is what diachronic time is, even and especially in the tradition that Levinas himself belonged to and esteemed. For, wasn't the work of world-making in the Hebrew Bible followed by a sacred day, positively non-productive and non-reproductive, the day of rest? Diachrony between the six days of creation and Sabbath is the temporalization of time. Sabbath: the blossoming of the divine flower, gifted to everything that lives, grows, produces and reproduces, plays.

---

38   Levinas, *Totality and Infinity*, p. 268.
39   Levinas, *Totality and Infinity*, p. 268.

CHAPTER 5

This Plant Who Is a Ghost: Vegetal Anachronies

When a specter haunts, who or what returns? In what way? Is it the form of a bygone existence? A pale afterglow of its content? The mind or the body? Or does something of the relation between them survive its dissolution, tense and fragile as that relation may have been in the lifetime?

The revenant is ethereal, but we often imagine it as having a shape, vaguely reminiscent of a silhouette, which used to belong to the deceased. Typically, this shape is human. Occasionally, it is recognizable as an animal.[1] And what about plants? Is the fact they do not seem to merit the status of specters not a symptom of their exclusion from the realm of spirit (materially: from breath; and ideally, from the domain of all that is venerable in Western thought)? Can a plant haunt? Does it ever return, and, if so, from where?

Whatever the outlines of a ghostly figure, the logic driving its apparitions is rigorously animalistic. An organism perishes as a whole and, thereafter, its spiritual form, too, returns as a whole, projecting a past that seems to have been irretrievably lost into the future. It comes back as an ideal unity of vitality that pulled together and bestowed meaning upon the material substratum of life.[2] The difference is that, in its comeback, it is devoid of such a substratum, proving that material existence is not essential to the survival of spiritual (here, ghostly) essence.

Organismic life and death are consistent with animality and with the logical principle of noncontradiction, admitting no middle states. The revenant's silhouette is a trace of mortal totality that complicates this bifurcation after the end, rather than in the middle, of a life. Pure organism, separate from its tissues

---

1　Think back in this respect to Sir Arthur Conan Doyle's *The Hound of the Baskervilles*, inspired by the posthumous legend of Squire Richard Cabell, whose ghost was periodically spotted leading a phantom pack of hounds.

2　"The animal is the existent idea in so far as its members are purely and simply moments of the form, perpetually negating their independence and bringing themselves back into their unity, which is the reality of the notion and is for the notion. If a finger is cut off, it is no longer a finger, but a process of chemical decomposition sets in. In the animal, the fully achieved unity is for the implicit unity, and this latter is the soul (*Seele*), the notion, which is present in the body in so far as this is the process of idealization" (Hegel, *Philosophy of Nature*, p. 352). "The animal organism is the microcosm, the center of nature, which has achieved existence for itself in which the whole of inorganic nature is recapitulated and idealized" (Hegel, *Philosophy of Nature*, p. 356).

© MICHAEL MARDER, 2024 | DOI:10.1163/9789004679894_007

and organs, viscera and limbs, is a ghost, a shadow of its material self without anything or anyone casting this shadow.[3] The return of pure organism signals both its idealization—the reiteration of the same being bereft of a material shell—and its contamination—a hovering in the excluded middle between life and death. Pure organism is the ghost that, colloquially and humorously speaking, we "give up" when we die, the metaphysical matrix of biophysical reality, gathered into a hierarchical organic unity.

If the return of pure organism is the principle of spectral logic, then plants do not fit the bill: they neither live as an organismic totality nor do they die all at once. Cutting a limb of a tree off is not the same as severing a member of an animal or a human. A plant's members or organs as not "simply moments of its form," and, as such, their independence is not perpetually negated but reinstated when the ecological conditions are propitious to their regrowth. Basic biological and physiological data suggest that there is no pure vegetal organism, no "implicit unity," from which to deduce a coherent plant subjectivity and, therefore, no kind of ghostly return of pure organism that is associated with animal or human hauntings. Nevertheless, the patchy nature of plant life and death need not bar flowers, trees, shrubs, and even grasses from joining the ranks of ghosts. Quite the opposite: at its most intense, spectrality is vegetal.

Instead of the organismic principle distilled from the actual organism and capable of outliving an organic body, whose shape it vaguely recalls, plants live in a way that is originally impure, cross-contaminated with life and death. The confluence of life and death in the "same" space and time of existence supports the hypothesis regarding the vegetal nature of spectrality. The collective being that is a plant consists of living, dying, and dead members. Its kingdom is as much *bio*logical as it is *thanato*logical.[4] More to the point, vegetal life is haunted by vegetal death: it lives off the decaying and decayed plants turned into compost, including (in the case of a tree) its own fallen leaves and fruits. In the materiality of existence, such a haunting is nothing "spooky"; it does not pose a threat to the living, whom it provides with the necessities of life. An inconspicuous ghostly dimension is the crossroads of growth and decay that traverse all forms of existence, not just that of plants.

---

3 In this sense, to die is to "give up the ghost," which does not preclude the return of the ghost one has given up after the instant of death.

4 While *nekros* is peppering contemporary discursive formations (necro-politics, necro-epistemology, etc.), *thanatos* is nowhere to be found. The figuration, the process, and the event of death indicated by the latter are unthinkable, especially compared to the already dead matter implied by the former. Yet, if plants are figurations of time, they are the *figures* of life and death—hence, of *thanatos* rather than *nekros*.

The ideal principle of existence, or the absence thereof, has to do not only with being but also with the time of existents. Along with animal subjectivity, the time of the animal (and even more so of the human) is idealized and totalized by the logic of pure organism. Whether as a circle or a line striving to infinity, the abstract geometrical models of time are traces of this idealization. Granted: in the course of a haunting comeback and its anachronic implications, abstract models are disrupted or put "out of joint," as Derrida writes echoing Shakespeare. Extreme idealization de-idealizes itself; organismic purity lapses into the impurity of life-and-death in its ghostly separation from the mortal organism. In the case of plants, however, none of the abstract models applies, because there is no total form of being or of time to be panoramically overviewed when facing vegetal existence. The time of plants is figured, configured, continuously reconfigured, and *unformed*.

The configured absence of a coherent form outstrips the limits of vegetal temporality; it pertains to the vegetality of time itself. Separations between different classes or types of beings and times are tentative: every kind of life is haunted by vegetal death. Receiving nourishment from animal or plant flesh, we metabolize the rot and the sun that fed plants that fed animals in a shorter or longer chain of ghostly transformations.[5] It is due to something over and above (or below) life *in* vegetal life that plants nevertheless spook us and are represented as zombie-like in horror films and fiction.[6] Human and non-human animals likewise contain traces of death in life, but their hiddenness from sight means that they come back to disturb the living *after* their demise. The enlivening and yet morbid underside of life is more obviously contemporaneous with life, more accentuated, its demarcations starker, in plants. The contemporaneity of life and death is the unhinging of time in time configured without a unified settled form, the anarchy of time that, in a shorthand of sorts, is called *spectrality*.

• • •

Seeds are tiny specters waiting on the sidelines of time to make their comeback, without any guarantees of it materializing. Each of them is a trace of the

---

5   In his reading of Mauss, Derrida recognizes, formally and rather *en passant*, the connection between spectrality and nourishment [Jacques Derrida, *Donner le temps 1: La fausse monnaie* (Paris: Éditions Galilée, 1991), p. 146]. Since nourishment belongs under the heading of the Aristotelian vegetal soul, this connection is yet another link between spectrality and vegetality.

6   See, for instance, the collection *Plant Horror: Approaches to the Monstrous Vegetal in Fiction and Film*, edited by Dawn Keetley & Angela Tenga (New York & London: Palgrave Macmillan, 2016).

past that may flourish in the future, and so is every moment of time itself. Dried or deep-frozen, seeds may delay the renaissance of the plant they issued from by hundreds of years. For example, the longevity of the *Canna compacta* seeds, found in a tomb in the high Andes, has been estimated at six hundred years.[7] Between their release from the mother plant's pod or cone and the instant of their germination that may never arrive, they linger in the grey area of living death. From there, they haunt the possibilities of survival, capable of overturning the historical verdict, condemning their species to extinction. Seed banks are vegetal séances institutionalized, the communities of ghosts, rather than the sites for accumulating natural capital condensed in vegetal DNA.

The outlook for germination can be seasonal, *or* it can exceed regular time constraints altogether. The temporality of time seethes in this excess. To be disseminated, spread perhaps for nothing, the seed does not need to be wasted: it disseminates itself, all by itself. Its dissemination, moreover, is that of the instant, of a temporal point that does not coincide with itself, even in the apparent calm and non-eventfulness of its self-identity. The instant haunts; bypassing the present, the seed and the event are the hauntings of the future with a possible past. The specters populating the sidelines of time *are* time.

At least since Aristotle, the relation between a seed and a fully developed plant—between a germ and its mature elaboration—has been the preferred paradigm of potential and actual being. It is this old metaphysical scheme that still performs much of the theoretical work behind the scenes of Hegel's philosophy of nature and that affects the notion of time, in which a seed is analogous to the point of an instant. But, already in a vegetally inflected teleology, anachrony is unavoidable: in the future of germination, it is the past that is awaiting us after an indeterminate and often unlimited delay of its reemergence. So, a key difference is not between anachrony and synchrony, but, rather, between a negative teleological judgment passed on the non-fruition of the potential in the actual, on the one hand, and thrill with the eventful delay and its unexpected hauntings, on the other.

One kind of disruption in the teleological scheme is the non-fulfillment of the potential inherent to a given class of beings, leading to what I am tempted to call *objective disappointment*. A "'seedless' fruit is in a sense imperfect," states Aristotle in *Metaphysics* (1023a), taking "perfection" to mean living up to one's appropriate purpose or end (*telos*) and neglecting the nutritive value of this fruit for animals or the contribution of its rotting away to the enrichment

7 J. Derek Bewley, et al., *Seeds: Physiology of Development, Germination and Dormancy*, 3rd Edition (New York & Heidelberg: Springer, 2013), p. 343.

of the soil—ends that are not autotelic, that do not immediately close the circle of self-relation. Though it is supposed to harbor reproductive potentiality, of which a seedless fruit is an empty sign, the barren plant does not put this power into action, does not actualize it. To cope with objective disappointment, such non-actualization is dismissed as a mere accident, a random deviation from the normal course of events, a singular instance when things do not work, that is, are not all that they could be. Seen through a deconstructive lens, the same non-arrival of being at its intended destination is the *sine qua non* for the event, making room for possibility (and impossibility) within the otherwise closed circuit of potentiality and actuality. Non-fulfillment, non-germination, or non-fruition betoken the opening and openness of time in a manner that is not to be conflated with the ideology of progress and *its* dissimulated, disingenuous teleology.

Another sort of disruption is due to the attribution of the potential (*dunamis*) of one type of being to another. Since animal capacities are superadded onto and presuppose those of plants, and those of humans are superadded onto and presuppose those of plants and animals, chances are that the non-fulfillment of "higher" capacities will leave animals and humans with those of the "lower" ones, belonging to plants. Failure to actualize our potentiality for thinking, in accordance with the principle of non-contradiction, demotes us, as Aristotle writes, precisely to the level of plants: "If, however, all men alike are both right and wrong, no one can say anything meaningful; for one must then at the same time say these and also other things. And he who means nothing, but equally thinks and does not think, in what respect does his condition differ from that of a plant?" (*Metaphysics* 1008b). Just as, ontologically, the event happens when something becomes possible outside the logic of potentiality, so, epistemologically, it comes to pass when one thinks outside the dictates of formal logic. That is to say, one thinks in and with time, with life-death, growth-decay, vegetal existence.

Even in the extreme of a perfect and complete fulfilment of potentialities, hauntings do not cease; temporal movement and temporalization do not come to a halt. The future of sensation and perception and cognition comes to us from the vegetal past of nourishment and reproduction that are, to be sure, replete with their own discernments, perceptions, and decision-making capacities. Becoming actual, potentiality becomes other to itself *as an actuality*; successfully germinating, the seed becomes other to itself as a shoot; as *ousia* or *parousia*, the fulness of presence, the instant becomes other to itself in the completion of time in time. Potentiality, the future of the past, is not consumed wholesale in its passages into the present, in which it is lost as a potentiality in the very moment of its fulfillment. Actuality, the shoot, and presence are haunted by the potentialities that they were, the potentialities that they will have continued to be, otherwise. Nor is potentiality ever pure. Upon a closer look, it reveals that it has an actual body in the world, or, as Aristotle puts it: "There is always something already there, out of which the resultant thing comes; for instance, the seed of a plant or animal" (*Physics* 190b). The seed *qua* potentiality is an actual potentiality, while its actualization is a potential or a potentiated actuality. Each instant, too, is both at once: an actual potentiality and a potential actuality, a seed and a shoot, a point and a linear limit, itself and the other.

The something that is already there at the bare minimum of potentiality is more than what appears in the theoretical focus of a philosopher. The *dunamis* of plants is both internal, or genetically constituted, and external, distributed among a congeries of environmental conditions and circumstances that co-determine the actual look of a sapling. This surplus is ghostly. That is why Hegel misses the point when he concentrates on the vegetal point, the seed, apparently containing in itself all there is to be expected from a plant, just "in miniature": "The development of the germ [*Samenkorn*] is at first mere growth, mere increase; it is already in itself the whole plant, the whole tree, etc., in miniature. The parts are already fully formed, receive only an enlargement, a formal repetition, a hardening, and so on."[8] In fact, growth is never "mere growth," never a mere quantitative increase, but a complex negotiation between the growing plant and its milieu, as well as, within some plants, between the phases of vegetative growth and sexual reproduction. In other words, growth is haunted and it is a haunting.

Passages from actual potentiality to potential potentiality (and back) are, likewise, anything but smooth. Even when successfully traversed, they are punctuated by pauses, glitches, and transcription errors. Actualization proceeds in tandem with de-actualization, disturbing the scheme of a preordained teleological sequence. Delays are not mere deferrals of the inevitable; they potentialize potentiality as such. Not limited to the interval between various steps, they constitute some of these steps, including seeds. A seed is the delay of its germination; a shoot is a delay of a mature plant; a bud is a delay of the flower; a flower is a delay of the fruit; a fruit is a delay of the seed (and within the fruit, its unripe stage is a delay of ripeness, supported by a complex biochemical apparatus that, in the meanwhile, discourages the attention of animals[9]). In other words, each instant is a delay of its own actualization—not only in the sense of affording enough time for processes to run their course, but also in the sense of the not-enough or never-enough of time in the midst

8   Hegel, *Philosophy of Nature*, p. 323.
9   Hallé, *In Praise of Plants*, 166.

of its finitude. For something to happen, to take place, it cannot happen all at once. Were it not for the delays of time, the delays that are time, everything in its simultaneity would have amounted to nothing. This, perhaps, is the ideational basis for what Kant rushly reduced to the successive nature of time, which is not, unlike space, "all at once."

Understood in terms of delay, the seed and the instant are points of energetic rest, of disengagement on the hither side of the usual distinction between activity and passivity. Time is the time of disengagement, which does not preclude a sudden re-engagement, an irruption experienced as a haunting, a ghostly return. Freud's fragmentary theory of time bears out this notion. In his famous essay on "The 'Mystic Writing-Pad'," Freud reiterates the argument about the atemporal nature of the unconscious, which utilizes the system of perception-consciousness (*Pcpt.-Cs.*) to probe the world outside: "It is as though the unconscious stretches out feelers, through the medium of the system *Pcpt.-Cs.*, toward the external world and hastily withdraws them as soon as they have sampled the excitations coming from it. Thus [...] the actual breaking of contact which occurs in the Mystic Pad was replaced in my theory by the periodic non-excitability of the perceptual system. I further had a suspicion that this discontinuous method of functioning of the system *Pcpt.-Cs.* lies at the bottom of the origin of the concept of time."[10]

Time originates in the discontinuity of engagement, or in "the periodic non-excitability of the perceptual system." Rather than an unending flux, time begins when something that was under way stops: it is the synergy of the ongoing and the intermittent, of the "always already," countless ends, and new beginnings. On the conceptual plane, it peers out of and retreats into the timeless, corroborating Plato's insight into time as "a moving image of eternity [*kinēton tina aiōnos*]" (*Timaeus* 37d). The "feelers," which the unconscious extends toward the outside world through conscious perceptions and representations as its means, are simiar to the animal or plant organs for exploring the immediate surroundings. Their approaching and retracting rhythms shape time in Freud's psychoanalysis. A fresh approach following a retraction is ghostly, a more or less unexpected return of what seems to have disappeared. Just as ghostly is lying in wait, the timeless vigilance of the unconscious that, for the time being (which is the being of time), does not give any outer signs of excitability. The seed and the instant, the point and a potentiality that keeps in reserve neither regulatively or constitutively anticipating another

---

10   Sigmund Freud, "The Mystic Writing-Pad." In *The Ego and the Id and Other Works*, Standard Edition, Vol. XIX (1923–1925), edited by James Starchey, et al. (London: Vintage Classics, 2001), p. 231.

actuality—these are the facets of retraction, of a break and disengagement that instigate the movement of time.

• • •

The spectrality of seeds is nothing ethereal; it can be as banal and mundane as their relation to waste and digestion.[11] One of the mechanisms of seed dispersal is their transportation in the stomachs and intestines of birds and other animals and their subsequent excretion in another locale than the one where the seed was ingested.[12] The indigestible outer kernel of the seed ensures its integrity throughout the process, while the period of time between ingestion and excretion—another instance of a temporalizing delay—permits seeds to be spread farther away from their initial site.

Aristotle cuts the association of seeds with potentiality in *De partibus animalium*, where he transforms them into waste, a byproduct of vegetal nutrition. He does so by announcing a "rebeginning," *archēs palin*, of the entire investigation, a regrowth or a haunting reflux to the "first things," *apo tōn prōtōn* (655b29), "first" not in the order of time but in the order of the metaphysics and the "first philosophy" of the living. Those "first things" are not abstract principles, but food, digestion, and the elimination of waste—things that are, not coincidentally, relevant to the nutritive power or the vegetal soul, *to threptikon*, and to the material infrastructure of time and temporalization. According to Aristotle, animals "of perfect formation," *teleiois*, have organs responsible for the intake of food and for excretion; plants that, by implication, are not perfect or have an ontologically damaged relation to the *telos*, have no equivalent to the intestine and are "without any part for the discharge of waste residue." "For the food which they absorb from the ground," Aristotle continues, "is already concocted before it enters them, and instead they give off as its [this residue's, MM] equivalent their fruit and seeds" (655b33–38).

As is so often the case with contemplating vegetal phenomena and dynamics, the most essential turns out to be the most superfluous, and vice versa: the potentialities of seeds and fruits flip into excretable residue.[13] In the Aristotelian

---

11   In turn, and to invert things a little, specters may be considered as the unwastable part of waste, the return of the one who or that which appears to have been thoroughly wasted away, absorbed by death, digested into the body of the earth and into the other elements—but not completely, never completely.

12   Hallé, *In Praise of Plants*, 163.

13   A little earlier in the same text, Aristotle states that "plants get their food from the earth by their roots; and since it is already treated and prepared no residue is produced by plants—they use the earth and the heat in it instead of a stomach, whereas practically all animals, and unmistakably those that move about from to place to place, have a stomach,

text itself, the sense of seeds is haunted by its other, by its counter-sense, which completes it, namely useless residue, waste. Not to be forgotten is also the idea that, while the nutritive-reproductive power originates and is exhaustive in the psychic life of plants, it is one that is equally indispensable to all living beings. The time of the living is thus rooted in the time of nutrition and reproduction, that is to say, the time of reproduction in oneself and in the other. All other temporalities are derivative, haunted by their material psycho-physiological substratum.

A mutated version of the Aristotelian line of thought, with the barely noticed vegetal undertones to do with *to threptikon*, runs from Augustine ("We might say that memory is a sort of stomach for the mind, and that joy or sadness are like sweet or bitter food"[14]) to Hegel, Nietzsche, and Derrida, who completes this venerable lineage by inverting it into the indigestible and the inassimilable. The lack of stomach and intestine analogues in plants—a nourishment without nourishment, digestion without digestion—implies in this scheme their tethering to a food source, a continuous flow of nourishment, and, therefore, a time without time, a time without delays, breaks, and intermittencies. Spatial restraints are the corollaries of a fledgling temporality, a time as of yet unwon from uninterrupted feeding and marked by a lack of independence.

Still with reference to the length and width of the intestine, Aristotle transposes the difference between plants and animals onto a distinction within the animal kingdom: "In those animals, however, which have to be more controlled in their feeding, there are no great wide spaces in the lower gut, but their intestine is not straight, as it contains many convolutions. Spaciousness in the gut causes a desire for bulk of food, and straightness in the intestine makes the desire come on again quickly. Hence, animals of this sort are gluttonous: those with simple receptacles eat at very short intervals of time, those with spacious ones eat very large quantities" (675b22–28). Temporalization is related to

---

or bag—as it were, an earth inside them—and in order to get the food out of this [...] they must have some instrument corresponding to the roots of a plant" (650a15-2). The earth, in which plants are rooted does not disappear from animal digestion; in addition to the plants' mediations between the world of the minerals and animals, this earth "as it were" is inside the animal as nourishment, gradually transformed into waste. As an animal, one is rooted in oneself, psychically and physiologically, even if this rootedness is mediated by the other. Hence, again: "The roots of plants are of course in the ground [*tēn gēn*], because that is the source from which plants get their nutriment. For an animal, the stomach and the intestines correspond to the ground, the place from which the nutriment has to be derived" (678a12–14). Remarkably, Aristotle recognizes in these lines that even the elemental milieu of a plant (the earth) is still or already plant, despite the apparent end of the lower portion of plant bodies in root tips.

14   Saint Augustine, *Confessions*, translated by R.S. Pine-Coffin (London & New York: Penguin, 1961), p. 99.

vegetality in a diametrically opposed manner here: what replaces an indefinite, temporalizing delay of full actuality by the potentiality of the seed is the immediacy uninterrupted nourishment.[15] Said to exclude gaps of any kind, the time of plants and, to a lesser extent of "gluttonous" animals, is a pure present, an ongoing flow admitting no radical breaks between the modalities of time, no surprising returns of the past projected into the future, no hauntings.

In the subsequent history of Western thought, the Aristotelian regularization of nature with the help of seeds has proceeded largely unabated. Lucretius, for one, deduces the growth of each thing "from a fixed seed" (*De rerum natura*, 1.190). The seed is his ontological argument against creation *ex nihilo*, the event *par excellence*, which with its totally random and exceptional character would wreak havoc in the order of life, making plants to "suddenly spring up at unpredictable intervals and at unfavorable times of year" (1.181–2). Ovid associates primordial chaos with "the warring seeds of ill-matched elements," *discordia semina rerum* (*Metamophoses* I.9). Once the seeds of things are no longer ill-matched, elements can be freed from "the blind heap of things," set "each in its own place and bound fast in harmony" (I.24–25). Seeds come to serve as tools for erasing time in time, for reproducing the existing order as though there were no divergences between generations and nothing new, unexpected, or hauntingly forgotten cropped up at germination. The instant is also a means for doing away with time in time, for passing from the discrete to the continuity of the imperialistically extending, ever elongated, dominant present.

Regularity, predictability, reproducibility—qualities that are equally at the core of a valid scientific method—ensure control over regularized, predictable, and reproducible beings by maintaining control over time, by conjuring away the specter of a past and a future different from the present. The restoration of time, however, may be the work of a seed that genetically rebels against imposed homogeneity and of each moment that keeps the promise of divergence from the hegemonic present. This is the case of apple seeds that contain "the genetic instructions for a completely new and different apple tree, one that, if planted, would bear only the most glancing resemblance to its parents. If not for grafting—the ancient technique of cloning trees—every apple in the world would be its own distinct variety, and it would be impossible to keep a good one going beyond the life span of that particular tree."[16] Hinging upon

---

15   Novalis, too, attributed to the life plants (*das Leben der Pflanzen*) "an uninterrupted eating and fecundation [*ein unaufhörliches Essen und Befruchten*]" [Novalis, *Fragmentos de Novalis*, edited by Rui Chafes (Lisbon: Assírio e Alvim, 1992), p. 84], even though each of these activities—nourishment and sexual reproduction—is interrupted by the other, not to mention the many disruptions inherent to each of them taken separately.

16   Michael Pollan, *The Botany of Desire: A Plant's-Eye View of the World* (New York: Random House, 2002), p. 10.

heterozygosity, the incredible genetic variation that is embedded in apple seeds resists the efforts of domestication. The wild varieties that return after generations upon generations of grafts are the revenants of what could not be altogether suppressed. They are the irruptions of the instant, punctuating and puncturing the continuum of the present.

•••

If, as Derrida was fond of saying, a ghost is a host, who not only revisits a house after death but opens it up for habitation, then vegetal ghosts are the perfect hosts. That the planetary dwelling is at the very least vegetal indicates how everyone and everything else is received in it by plants, albeit not always in their immediate presence at the site of reception. On the evolutionary time-scale, plants are certainly older than animals—than the human animal, above all. Since the very first cyanobacteria that experimented with photosynthesis over two billion years ago and the symbiotic arrangement of these in prokary-otic cells "shortly" thereafter (about 150 million years subsequent to the emer-gence of cyanobacteria), plants have been shaping the atmosphere, aquatic and terrestrial ecosystems: they may be slotted into the category of revenants, the ghosts-hosts offering ecological hospitality to the present from the past, which comes back with and as them. And yet, such categorial differentiations are highly unstable, or, as Derrida writes, dealing with ghosts "will always keep one from discriminating among the figures of the *arrivant*, the dead, and the *revenant* (the ghost, he, she, or that which returns)."[17] The future of the event belongs together with the ghostly past.

The merging of the past and the future is characteristic of the spectral anachronies of time. The absolute *revenant* is also "the absolute *arrivant*," one who "surprises the host—who is not yet a host or an inviting power—enough to call into question, to the point of annihilating or rendering inde-terminate, all the distinctive signs of a prior identity, beginning with the very border that delineated a legitimate home and assured lineage, names and language, nations, families and genealogies."[18] Biological lineages and families included. *To threptikon*, the capacity for nourishment and reproduction in us is an instance of a surprising hosting, where it is by no means clear whether the human accommodates vegetal non-identity or the vegetal impercepti-bly lodges the human in the depths of what seems to be our psychic life. The caveat is that the surprising effect is achieved upon reflection and not so much

---

17   Jacques Derrida, *Aporias*, translated by Thomas Dutoit (Stanford: Stanford University Press, 1993), p. 35.

18   Derrida, *Aporias*, p. 34.

upon the sensory presentation of plants, which is largely taken for granted and barely acknowledged. With rare exceptions, such as the sudden dehiscence of a seed pod, their coming to appearance is not abrupt, in keeping with gradual and incomplete emergence at germination, compared to animal birth. Nor, therefore, is their reappearance or apparition startling.

The hospitality of plants in the milieu of life "renders indeterminate" the metaphysical distinction between the inside and the outside. They satisfy the material *a priori* condition of hospitality, namely to receive someone or something in the world, the condition potentiating the rest of the phenomenon and apparatus of hospitality in a country, a municipality, an apartment, or a room. To welcome into the world is to welcome into the open, rather than into the closure or the enclosure of a strictly bounded territory or a building. The vegetal mode of dwelling, which sustains the hospitality of plants, is congruent with the kind of energy regime that requires maximum exposure, as opposed to animal minimization of body surface for the efficiency of movement, heat preservation, etc. In this very precise sense, "our" dwelling is ensconced in and inhabited by its other, which is the other, vegetal project of dwelling. "Our" time, too, is nestled in and indwelt by the time of plants.[19]

In their company every single moment, whenever we breathe, we are breathing with plants. The very air we inhale is their expiration, the after-breath of trees and phytoplankton, kelp and algal plankton. The exteriority of the atmosphere entering the lungs is the vegetal specter in us. Given that, from Athens to Jerusalem, the ancients deemed the soul pneumatic, made of or related to air, this physiological fact is not trifling. The breath of life in Stoicism and in *Genesis* is a conduit from corporeal to spiritual reality, with vegetal, oxygen-generating respiration for a vanishing mediator, an elemental bridge suspended between these shores of being.

Dismissed by Church authorities as a heretic, the first-century Samaritan religious figure Simon Magus insisted that Paradise was the womb (*mētra*) of humanity, whereas Eden is the caul (*choríon*), enveloping the fetus,

---

19   The dwelling plants haunt, the ecology they dream up with their lives or deaths, is equally
      exterior, extraverted, stitched of uneven and disjunctive surfaces they gather together:
      rivers and mountains, fungi and bacteria, birds, butterflies, and bees, you and me. We are
      not the hostages of our vegetal hosts or ghosts (in *Aporias* Derrida draws the connections
      between ghosts, guests, hosts, hostages): instead of holding us inside a haunted house,
      they keep us in an adjacent unwalled garden, the garden without guarding, which we are
      actively changing into a barren, world-encompassing desert. This garden is the *oikos* of
      ecology, the house, from which humanity has been trying to escape from millennia by
      fabricating a closed dwelling for itself.

homophonous with the locality (*chōríon*), receiving existence into itself (Hippolytus, *Refutatio*, VI.14.8–10). The Paradisiac navel (*omphalos*) of the world acquires a literal shape on Simon's interpretation. The rivers of Paradise are veins and arteries transporting vital breath and nourishment to its inhabitants: they are the channels of spirit and breath, of breath as spirit (*ochetoi pneumatos*). This means that the trees of Paradise breathe for the human embryo, "for as it lay in the midst of moisture, at its feet was death, if it attempted to breathe; for it would thus have been drawn away from moisture and perished." A vegetal placenta breathes for humanity in its infancy, and it is doubtful that human breath can ever separate from this other-than-human womb, in which species and individual gestations alike happen.

Although Simon Magus does not spell this out, at least in the way his doctrine is sifted through Hippolyte's critical account of it, the Fall and expulsion from Paradise are tantamount to a separation and expulsion from the vital sources of our respiration. On the one hand, the expulsion may signify, simply, the process of mammalian birth with the subsequent cutting of the umbilical cord, albeit not of this or that individual human being, but of humanity as such. On the other hand, it may imply a loss of our vegetal roots, of a gestation that is more and other-than-animal, and of breathing and receiving nourishment from the plant world enveloping and permeating us. The first interpretation means that, after the moment of separation, human beings must learn to breathe and nourish themselves by themselves, without direct dependence on plants. But, particularly in this respect, the possibilities of physiological (and, hence, spiritual) autonomy are limited, since we cannot leave our vegetal placenta behind once and for all. The second interpretation is as unavoidable as it is charged with the progressively aggravating pathos of suffocation, of choking off vital air supply in the name of autonomy, maturity, and mastery. An anachronic struggle for breath ensues.

On the face of it, animal and vegetal kinds of breathing are the mirror opposites of one another: whereas plants exhale oxygen as a by-product of photosynthesis, animals exhale carbon dioxide. Rather than a mere opposition, the process is, however, dialectical. Animal breath, transpiring largely in the interiority of the bronchial tubes and the lungs, depends on plant respiration, which takes place out in the open, on the exposed surface of the leaf. Vegetative tissues release oxygen and CO_2 effluxes into the atmosphere, incorporating at the chemical or biochemical level the opposition between these two gases (as is also the case with virtually any other opposition) into themselves. Plants benefit to some extent from the carbon dioxide absorbed and converted into vegetal corporeality, but they do not require animal breath to maintain themselves alive. The Hegelian master-slave relation, observed on the horizon of what elsewhere I have called "material sustainability,"[20] is not what we take it to be in the anthropocentric sphere of instrumental rationality; in fact, the very oppositional categories of a master and a slave are appropriate to the formation of animal, not of vegetal, consciousness and its exaggeration in human self-consciousness. Ontic or ontological, a declaration of independence from the planetary placenta provided by plants is a non-starter, which, nonetheless, has been in a mindboggling manner guiding Western thought and history for millennia.

∙ ∙ ∙

Whatever shape it takes, breathing is not a continuous process with a constant rate of exchange of gases. Its rhythmicality, with all the variations and modulations, is decisive for time, for energy conversions, for life. The rhythms of breathing nicely exemplify the ghostly-pneumatic logic of time, subtly mediated by plants. With respect to breath, everything Derrida has to say on the subject of *hauntology* (the "logic of haunting" intimately bound, as its underside, to ontology) holds. "Repetition *and* first time: this is perhaps the question of the event as question of the ghost [*Répétition et première fois, voilà peut-être la question de l'événement comme question du fantôme*]. [...] Repetition *and* first time, but also repetition *and* last time, since the singularity of any *first time* makes of it also a *last time*. Each time it is the event itself, a first time is a last time. Altogether other. Staging for the end of history."[21] Everything is, admittedly, calmer with plants: there is no dramatic "staging for the end of history," but the interval between inhalation and exhalation, one breath or one birth and another, may be the last in the course of its repetitions and its singularity as first (again), as ever-recommencing. The event is mundane, somato-spiritual, vegetal-animal: breathing. Each instant, each seed, is a breath, split into two that contain three: inhalation-interval-exhalation; first-repetition-last; singular-airy-universal.

The asymmetries of the event point at the elephant, or the giant sequoia, in the room: the carbon footprint. Whose footprint is it? Who leaves it with what, or with whom? And in what substratum, where? *These* are today's "questions of the ghost." Burning fossil fuels, we conjure the specters of long-dead plants and

---

20   Michael Marder, "Sustainable Perspectivalism: Who Sustains Whom?" In Jack Appleton (ed.), *Values in Sustainable Development* (London & New York: Routledge, 2013), pp. 217–225.

21   Jacques Derrida, *Specters of Marx: The State of Debt, the Work of Mourning and the New International*, translated by Peggy Kamuf (New York & London: Routledge, 1994), p. 10.

prompt them to upend the breathing of the living, to choke existence itself. The combustion of natural gas, oil, or coal sets plants against plants. As the atmosphere fills with greenhouse gases, a spectral struggle ensues between the respiration that gives the gift of air and the exhausts that take it away. Before pneumatomachy can signify the denial of the divinity of the Holy Spirit, it names a battle over breath, for or against the possibility of breathing, in which the past of vegetal life is called upon to animate the present and anni-hilate the future.

The battle, in which the industrializing and the industrialized humanity takes the side of breathlessness, is aggravated by a drastic deforestation of the planet. In the current permutation of Western metaphysics, the breath of "objective spirit" is embodied in technology and extractive energy production—hence, paradoxically, in everything contributing to cutting breath off. At its behest, liquified, gasified or solidified organic matter is momentarily resurrected through massive combustion resulting in physical suffocation. The sublimated form of breath takes our breath away. The vegetal specter in our lungs is dou-ble: a specter and the specter *of* this specter, oxygen and carbon emissions, a past suffused with futurity and a futureless past.

A doubling, with mirroring effects between mutually exclusive elements, is the signature of the ghost, of spectral anachronies. The future intersects with the past and, in a further twist, the past bifurcates into pasts (two or more) and the future into the futures (two or more). This doubling, which is itself double to the power of n, teases out the non-identity of the self-identical, of the figureless figure of self-identity that is spirit: "The specter is *of the spirit*, it participates in the latter and stems from it even as it follows it as its ghostly double [*Le spectre est* de l'esprit, *il en participe, il en relève alors même qu'il le suit comme son double fantomal*]. The difference between the two is precisely what tends to disappear in the ghost effect."[22] That is why the denial of the spectrality of plants excludes them from the realm of spirit: to be a specter is to "participate" in spirit *and* to split away from it, following spirit as a double. But the inverse move, that of including plants, does not keep metaphysical spirit allergic to the work of time intact; spectrality, especially vegetal spectrality, is the temporalization of spirit.

Still on the subject of a historically conditioned vegetal spectrality, in *Spec-ters of Marx*, Derrida attends to a rather inconspicuous example of use-value, which Marx gives early on in volume 1 of *Capital*, namely a wooden table. "For example—and here is where the table comes on stage—the wood remains

---

22   Derrida, *Specters of Marx*, pp. 156–157.

wooden when it is made into a table: it is then 'an ordinary, sensuous thing [*ein ordinäres, sinnliches Ding*].' It is quite different when it becomes a commodity, when the curtain goes up on the market and the table plays actor and character at the same time."[23] As a commodity, the wooden table revives as an actor on the market; it then becomes "supernatural," "a *sensuous nonsensuous* thing."[24] How does this pervert the resurrection of the tree, of lumber out of which a table was made? Marx does not experience the ghostliness of the wooden table as wooden, the afterlife of a tree haunting "ordinary" use, a prototype of *material visitation*.[25] The spectrality of a commodity, in which a thing is redoubled into use- and exchange-values, will have been preempted by the material spectrality of the plants' posthumous survival—as air, food, fuel, clothes, paper, furniture, construction materials, and forth. The haunting is itself haunted, the doubling doubled: the times of use and exchange, of physiological functioning and cultural activities, of growths (vegetal and capital) involving and anachronistically interrupting each other.

With respect to Aristotelian existence "according to nature," *kata phusin*, the haunting is concentrated in a wooden bed frame, rather than a table. Citing Antiphon, Aristotle writes: "some hold that the nature and substantive existence of natural products resides in the material on the analogy of the wood of a bedstead or the bronze of a statue. Antiphon took it as an indication of this that if a man buried a bedstead and the sap in it took force and threw out a shoot [*blaston*], it would be tree and not bedstead that came up" (*Physics* II.I.193a10–15). Even an artefact can come alive again, if it is handed over to the earth: here, we have a case not of a *material visitation* but of *matter as*

---

23   Derrida, *Specters of Marx*, p. 188.

24   Derrida, *Specters of Marx*, p. 189.

25   "But whence comes the certainty concerning the previous phase, that of this supposed use-value, precisely, a use-value purified of everything that makes for exchange-value and the commodity-form? What secures this distinction for us? It is not a matter here of negating a use-value or the necessity of referring to it. But of doubting its strict purity. If this purity is not guaranteed, then one would have to say that the phantasmagoria began before the said exchange-value, at the thresh-old of the value of value in general, or that the commodity-form began before the commodity-form, itself before itself. The said use-value of the said ordinary sensuous thing, simple *hule*, the wood of the wooden table concerning which Marx supposes that it has not yet begun to dance,' its very form, the form that informs its *hule*, must indeed have at least promised it to iterability, to substitution, to exchange, to value; it must have made a start, however minimal it may have been, on an idealization that permits one to identify it as the same throughout possible repetitions, and so forth" (Derrida, *Specters of Marx*, p. 200). Derrida concentrates on the non-simplicity and hauntings of matter, of *hule*, that is derived from "wood" in Aristotelian thought. But he does not follow another trajectory, leading all the way back to the life of a tree.

visitation, with the possibility of life's reanimation after death (the death of a tree and its transformation into lumber). Matter's potentialities are indomitable, the *dunamis* that it is—not fully actualizable in any given form. What is experienced as a haunting, as the anachronic metamorphosis of dead wood into a living shoot, is this very excess of potentiality over the actual.

Contemporary pneumatomachy is a tragic afterglow of spectral doubling, which encompasses vegetal and animal dwelling in the world, ways of generating energy and value, exposure and retraction, a cultivation of interiority and synergy with the outside. The spectrality of these biological givens indicates that energy and time are not resources, dwelling is not a possession; they are what the living beings themselves are in the core or on the surface of their being. The genitive of specter that is, as Derrida writes, "of the spirit," *de l'esprit*, implies both a doubling of spirit (its non-identity in itself) and the spectre's world-making or world-unmaking role in the very materiality of existence, as that very materiality diffracted into unique patterns of energy, time, and being in the world.

The spectrality of vegetal life and death, futures and pasts, jointures, disjointures, and breaths is singular and generic, appropriate to plants and inviting other forms of life into its folds. In Derrida's words, "a spectral asymmetry interrupts here all specularity. It de-synchronizes, it recalls us to anachrony [*Elle désynchronize, elle nous rappelle à l'anachronie*]."[26] The asymmetry of the symmetric "singular and generic"—of the singular (time, energy, life) that is capaciously generic—matches the nutritive power of *to threptikon*, of reproduction in oneself and in the other, that is vegetal and other-than-vegetal. Its spectral visitations are the capacities to sense, to cognize, to represent, to imagine—in a word, psychic life (that beautiful mutation, the holding and the release, of breath) in all its aspects. *To threptikon* gathers and de-synchronizes parts of the psyche: it affords no panoramic view of what it fits together, no approach mediated by specularity, no spatially representable totality. Instead, it hands these bits over to time. When the co-belonging of the mutations of breath (and, in the first instance, of *to threptikon*) is felt, it is felt as the anachrony, the non- or de-synchronization of the vegetal with itself, its non-identity or non-self-identity *as* our identity. A doubling, and a doubling of this doubling, into the same and the other. Our lives and loves, thoughts and emotions, desires, appetites and judgments, economies and technologies, politics and art are so many trails of vegetal de-synchronization, the anachronic ghosts of plants.

---

26   Derrida, *Specters of Marx*, p. 6.

Excipit: Eleusinian Variations

To this day, very little is known about the Eleusinian Mysteries. Celebrated nearly every year between the sixth century BC and the end of antiquity,[1] these rituals were dedicated to the goddess of fertility Demeter and her daughter Persephone, abducted by the god of the underworld and imprisoned in Hades. In relative proximity to Athens, Eleusis was the place where Persephone reunited with her mother for a part of the year, before having to make an annual descent to the underworld, swathing the domain above ground in deep wintry grief.[2] The ceremonies of the Mysteries were complex, replete with different stages of initiation, long processions, fasts, and the drinking of a potion that was probably hallucinogenic. But, given that Demeter is the goddess of fertility, it is not far-fetched to assume that the Mysteries were a trace of the much older pre-Indo-European cultures and their "religions centered upon the female's procreativity and the cyclical re-birth and death of both plants and mankind."[3]

More than the content of the Eleusinian Mysteries, it is their ritualistic form that mattered. The Mysteries were passages: rites of passage or initiation, for sure, but also the transitions of plants and animals and humans from darkness to light, from death to birth, and back again. The ritual is a watershed moment that changes its participants from a *mustēs*, who "is a person with eyes closed and therefore blind to the truth," to an *epoptēs* who "sees the truth," if only with an intimate connection to darkness. Indeed, the word *mustērion*, which metamorphoses into the English "mystery," is related to the verbs *muō* ("to close my eyes or mouth") and *mueō* ("to make someone close their eyes or mouth").[4] In practical terms, too, the opening of one's eyes in the course of participation in Eleusinian Mysteries did not remove the blindfold or the gag once and for all: the reason for scant historical evidence about these rituals is that it was strictly prohibited, on the pain of death, to divulge to others what happened during festival days in Eleusis.

At the risk of an overgeneralization, it is possible to conclude that the Eleusinian Mysteries were an apprenticeship in becoming vegetal. Like

---

1   Michael Cosmopoulos, *Bronze Age Eleusis and the Origins of the Eleusinian Mysteries* (Cambridge: Cambridge University Press, 2015), p. 2.
2   Cosmopoulos, *Bronze Age Eleusis*, p. 8.
3   R. Gordon Wasson, Albert Hofmann, and Carl Ruck, *The Road to Eleusis: Unveiling the Secret of the Mysteries* (Berkeley: North Atlantic Books, 2008), p. 48.
4   Cosmopoulos, *Bronze Age Eleusis*, pp. 14, 15.

© MICHAEL MARDER, 2024 | DOI:10.1163/9789004679894_008

Persephone, plants live partly underground in the moist darkness of the soil and partly in the bright and airy expanse aboveground. Except that Persephone divides her time in these opposite abodes into various segments (corresponding to the seasons of the year when her mother, Demeter, is in mourning or joyfully vibrant) while plants live simultaneously above and below, in darkness and in light, descending and ascending. Becoming vegetal is converting succession into simultaneity without leaving the order of time: in the course of initiation rites into the Greater Mysteries in Eleusis that take place at the turning points of the seasons, time passes into space, its sequences condensed and presented all at once, and space is temporalized. Above and below, tapping into the reserves of consciousness and the unconscious, the *mustai* are living their deaths and dying to their lives, both dying and reborn in themselves. Their initiation cannot be an enlightenment, not only because, as described by Aristotle, it "was an emotional experience instead of a cerebral process of learning—*pathein* instead of *mathein*,"[5] but also because the gist of this initiation is an integration of light with darkness, of the sun with the soil, of shimmering life with the bustling obscurity of death.

The image-concept of time as a plant I have sketched on these pages belongs to the semantic constellation, in which the Greek *Mysteria* were encrusted thousands of years ago. Without experiencing it, without undergoing its unsettling effects, the process of learning about the vegetal nature of time would be vacuous. *Mathēsis* is insufficient unless it proceeds hand-in-hand with *pathos*—here and in all other matters. What does it mean to experience, viscerally, the truth of the statement "time is a plant"? Does it not compel us to discover, always respecting the entwinement of the luminous and the tenebrous, the vegetality of time within ourselves, all the way down or up to our consciousness, or what in phenomenology is called time-consciousness? Does it not move us to wonder about this figure of time outside ourselves, perhaps reducing to one the two things that, as Kant admitted, fill the mind with "admiration and awe," *Bewunderung und Ehrfurcht*?

The learning side of the process is also not to be neglected. In physics, relativity theory and quantum mechanics support the ultimately vegetal notions of spacetime configurations, reversibility, entanglement, the multiverse, and physical time realism. In plant sciences, studies of memory and anticipation, of the plants' phenomenological orientation in space and the measurements they take of changing daylight periods, offer clues to the sense of time from a vegetal standpoint. In contemporary philosophy and art, the subjectivity of

---

5   Cosmopoulos, *Bronze Age Eleusis*, p. 15.

plants, synergic and creative, molding and molded by the world, prepares the ground for the image-concept of time as a plant. This preparatory work has plenty to contend with, not least a deeply ingrained abstract framework of the transcendental aesthetic and the more recent anthropocentric paradigm of time-consciousness or of the existential analytic. Still, regardless of all the advances made in the arduous task of vegetalizing time, we will remain forever the initiates, the Eleusinian *mustai* in a life-long (and death-long) apprenticeship with plants.